OLD DAYS ON THE PRAIRIE

TOM KILIAN

OLD DAYS ON THE PRAIRIE

BY
TOM KILIAN

Copyright © 2007 by Tom Kilian

All rights reserved. No part of this book may be reproduced or utilized in any form or by any means, electronic or mechanical, including photocopying, recording, or by any information storage and retrieval system, without permission in writing from the publisher. Inquiries should be addressed to Tom Kilian, 2700 South Jefferson Avenue, Sioux Falls, South Dakota 57105.

Library of Congress Control Number: 2007940181

ISBN: 978-1-57579-367-2

Cover photos by Joel Strasser, Paul Horsted, David Ode and James Kilian.

Printed in the United States of America

PINE HILL PRESS
4000 West 57th Street
Sioux Falls, SD 57106

DEDICATION

Mabel Amanda and Ward Van Kilian

Ward and Mabel Kilian lived their lives quietly without fanfare or public notice. They endured some of the most difficult challenges that life can offer. They were idealists who believed in the best in people. They were honest, open, and committed to goodness. Their patience and abiding strength served as an encouragement to many. They were the finest parents one could hope for.

ACKNOWLEDGEMENTS

Many people helped in many ways to provide information, verify facts and give encouragement to the writing of this book.

Special thanks are due to Tami Severson for editorial help and electronic transcription of the manuscript and to Joe Mierau of Pine Hill Press for technical help in production.

For photography, I am indebted to Joel Strasser, Paul Horsted, David Ode, James Kilian, Arlein Fransen, Doris Hill, Chad Coppess of South Dakota Tourism, Harry Thompson of the Center for Western Studies, Augustana College and many anonymous early photographers who recorded events of the past. To Jeannette Kommes for her remarkable skills in photo enhancement and layout and for research in locating early photos, I owe sincere thanks.

Thanks are due to the staff of the Miner County Pioneer, to Phyllis Lauer, Leta Trusty and Lulu Anderson of the Miner County Rural Life Museum and to Charlene Sundstrom of the Miner County Clerk of Courts office.

Appreciation and thanks go to Randy Parry for his astonishing attainments in building the Miner County Community Revitalization (MCCR), in reshaping Miner County and without whom this book probably would never have been undertaken.

To my wife, Lorna, lifetime companion, encourager and friend, thanks for countless hours of editing the materials of this book.

CONTENTS

I. VILAS
THE TOWN..1
THE LANDMARKS 8
HEAR THE TRAIN BLOW 34
THE TOWN SITE WAR 46

II. LIFE IN AND AROUND VILAS
THE KILIANS IN VILAS 49
EARLY AMERICANA..52
THE ROCK CREEK STAGE STATION 55
EARLY RADIO..59
SLING SHOT HEY – DAY 62
THE RUBBER GUN WARS...64
THE ERFMAN TRAGEDY...66
READ, WRITE AND CIPHER 68
THE METHODIST CHURCH.......................................77

III. FARMING
THE FAMILY FARM 79
THE HAY MAKERS..83
THE THRESHERS...86
THE CORN HUSKERS 95
THE PLAGUES OF THE 1930's 99
THE GREAT DEPRESSION 109

IV. HOLIDAYS
    MAY DAY 113
    THE FOURTH OF JULY 114
    HALLOWEEN HORROR 119
    THANKSGIVING 121
    CHRISTMAS 122
    WINTER PLAY FOR KIDS 126

V. THE PRAIRIE IN MINER COUNTY
    THE NATURAL PRAIRIE 131
    SLOUGHS AND WETLANDS 134
    WILDFIRES 137
    EARLY ROADS 140
    CRICKET-CHIRPING NIGHTS 144
    THE CYCLONES OF SUMMER 146
    THE BLIZZARDS OF WINTER 150

VI. PRAIRIE LIFE
    STALKING THE STRIPED GOPHER 155
    ROCK CREEK BULLHEADS 161
    CLOTHING 166
    WATER 170
    WHAT'S FOR DINNER 174
    THE PARTY LINE 181
    GYPSY CARAVANS 183
    ITINERANT PEDDLERS 186
    COMMUNITY DANCES 188
    BOOTLEGGERS 190
    TWIN LAKES 191
    SATURDAY NIGHTS IN HOWARD 194

FOREWORD

This book is not intended as a careful history, though hopefully, it is accurate. Most of the accounts are intended as a general portrait of what was going on in Miner County and in the village of Vilas in the period of time between the first and second World Wars. Think of these two wars as bookends, holding this span of time between them.

The book is a collection of places and events in an attempt to recapture the flavor and feel and sense of what life was like in the years from about 1920 to 1940. Life was very different then – so much so that anyone born after the second World War can hardly imagine it or understand it. This book may help.

For the history to become real, one must recreate the setting, the feel and smell of the times in which events occurred. One must try to detail the backdrop that the times provided.

This book is not intended as an autobiography, though it becomes one to a degree, since one's recollections place him in the action. The times, the events, the commonly-held ideas and social norms of the period must certainly have helped to shape me. In a larger sense, it may help some people understand the region better, how it evolved as it has and why people now believe and behave as they do.

In my view, the period between the wars was a major divide for America. The two decades before World War II were literally a different world: people seemed more simple and trusting, more open and courteous, less driven and intense. Life moved at a much slower pace. Speed in everything was much less. It was a more relaxed and peaceful and happy time. The nation and the world were much larger and places were more distant and more filled with wonder. I hope this book can reflect some of that world.

The reader may find assertions or descriptions that are not what others might recall. I may have misplaced events or misspelled names or otherwise created offense. If so, please forgive; I meant well.

THE TOWN OF VILAS

THE TOWN

The planners of the town of Vilas had great expectations for its future: when they surveyed the site in August 1883, they drew up a plat that was about three times the size of Howard and up to ten times the size of any other county town site. The site was made possible by the extension of the Chicago, Milwaukee, St. Paul and Pacific Railroad as it built to the west across the county. There were two additions to the original plat of Vilas, one later in 1883 and another in 1888. It was located about 3 1/2 miles west of Howard in almost the exact center of the county. The town site was fixed by the decision of the Chicago, Northwestern Railroad to intersect the Chicago, Milwaukee at that point.

Because Vilas had two railroads in 1883, there was reason for optimism among the early settlers. In those times, railroads were everything and for a small village to have two lines was an unthinkable wonder. Locals announced Vilas as "the railroad center of Miner County" and great things were expected.

Like most prairie villages, the main street was called Main Street where almost all of the businesses of consequence were located. The Vilas Main Street ran east and west parallel to the present Highway #34, which runs about three to four blocks south of it. The street was graveled and had cement sidewalks along the north side, which ran the length of the town, about a half mile, end to end.

In the 1930's, moving east along the north side of Main Street, the following businesses were operating or still standing: Bill Hepner's Store and Post Office, Frank Wynn's Pool

Hall and Ice Cream Parlor, the Gehring Hotel, John Hepner's Store, the Northwestern Railroad Depot, DeHaven's Stockyards and Anderson's Store. There were family homes and vacant lots interspersed between the buildings on both sides of the street.

On the south side of the street were: Frank Bernstetter's Garage, the Independent Order of Odd Fellows (IOOF) Hall, Ross Sweeney's Cream Station, the blacksmith shop, the livery barn, Raymond's Land Office and the Northwestern Railroads, coal sheds.

South of the Post Office on Main Street, toward the highway, were coal sheds, a lumber yard, a large grain elevator operated by Carl Larson and the depot and sheds of the Milwaukee Railroad.

On the north side, about a block north of the hotel was the Town Pump, which consisted of a steel-towered wind mill, an iron pump and a small water tank. Several blocks to the east were the Northwestern Railroad's water tower and the extensive pens and chutes of the DeHaven Stockyards.

The public school building, housing both the elementary and high schools, and the Methodist Church were located on the northwest edge of the town, about two blocks west and two or three north of the Post Office.

Every building in the entire town was a wooden frame building, mainly painted white, with a few light greys and browns. There were no village-owned utilities – all water was from individual wells and cisterns; all electric power was from a private company. There were no sewer or waste treatment facilities and every private home had an outhouse. There was no garbage or trash collection system; householders and businesses alike either burned or buried their rubbish on their own land.

There were a few electric street lights up and down Main Street but none on the dirt side streets, which were little more than public rights of way. Streets were maintained by a road

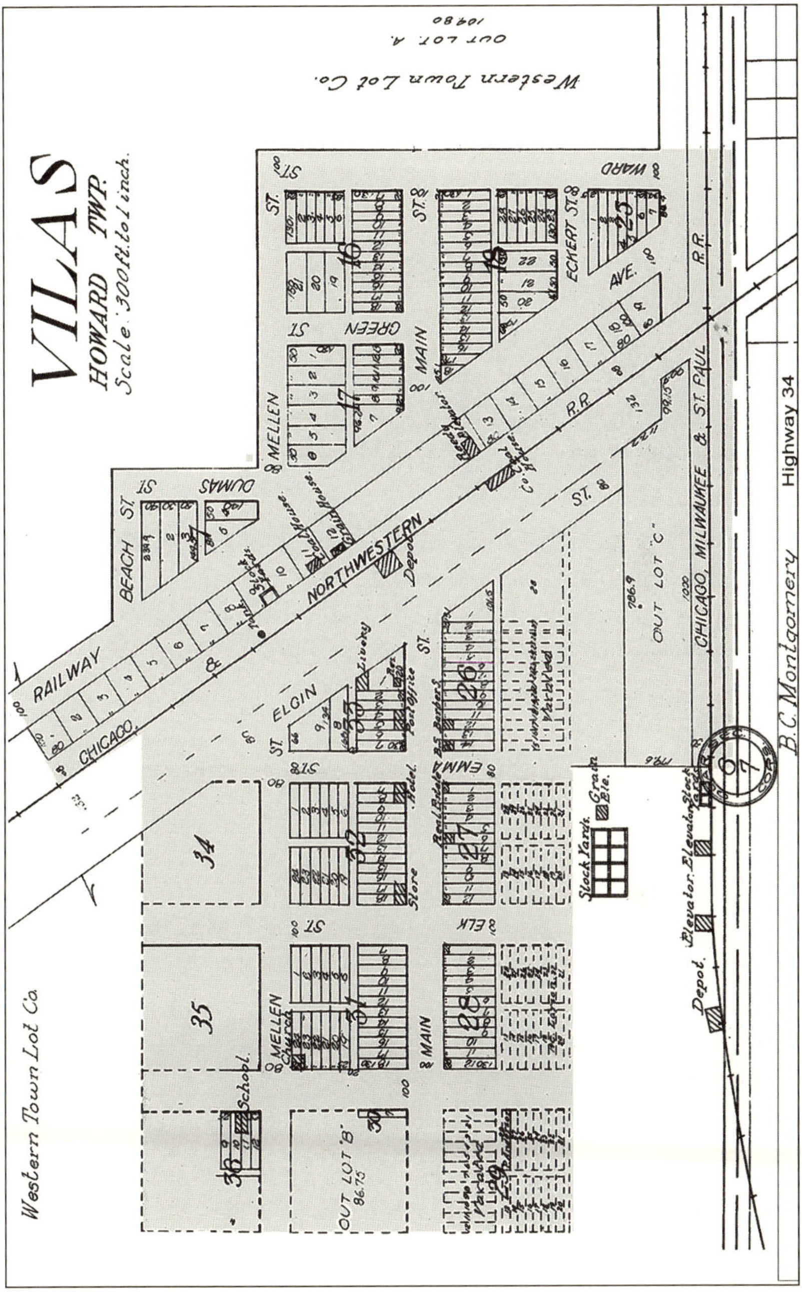

Main Street of Vilas, north side, west end of town.

Main Street, south side showing the Cream Station and Blacksmith Shop.

grader; pulled by horses, to level the ruts left by wet weather. There were no public parks or parking areas and no need for them. In earlier times, the town was larger with a population of perhaps 400. There had been many more small businesses to include several newspapers, grain elevators, hotels and banks but most had already vanished to accommodate the changing times. The Vilas State Bank, the last remaining one, liquidated its assets and paid off its creditors in 1927.

It had been over forty years since the town was laid out in 1883, when land boomer enthusiasm ran high. Rapidly growing technology had already worked profound changes in the prairie society and there was no longer a need for a "full service community" every five or six miles along the way.

Town business conducted on the public's behalf, was handled by a village board and by the school board. There was little to oversee, except maintaining streets, mowing grass and weeds along the roads and street lighting. Law enforcement was in the hands of the county sheriff and he was rarely seen or needed.

The first government survey of township borders and section lines was in progress north of Vilas in 1871 – twelve years before the railroads reach the area. All the farms around Vilas and in all of Miner County were first owned as a result of land claims filed by early settlers. There were three major programs under which the Federal government would permit all settlers to claim land:

1) The Preemption Act of 1841 permitted settlers to locate a claim of 160 acres and after six months of residency and cultivation of the land, to purchase it for $1.25 an acre.

2) The Homestead Act of 1862 allowed a claim of 160 acres if the settler lived on the land for six months each of the next five years. In addition, if the settler paid a fee of $1.25 an acre, he could convert the

claim to being one under the Preemption Act. This then allowed him to take up another additional claim under the Homestead Act, giving him a total of 320 acres.

3) The Timber Culture Act of 1873 and as amended in 1878, allowed a claim of 160 acres if the settler planted 2700 trees on 10 acres of the land. In order to prove up the claim and receive a patent, he had to be able to show at least 675 live trees.

Following the granting of the original claims, many things happened so that ownership was transferred to later owners. Some claims were abandoned by the first settlers, who found the life too demanding. Some claims were sold to settlers who followed. Some were lost to commercial agencies through foreclosures on loans against the land.

It was said that Matthew Moore who owned the original site that became the town of Howard, received land under all three of these land claim programs!

The "dwellings" that most settlers built on the land claims were simple, modest places in the extreme. They were usually small, one room structures, built of boards or sometimes, of sod, plowed up on the site. They were covered on the outside with tar paper, which was tacked down with thin wooden laths. The roofs were of boards, usually sloped in one direction. There were one or two very small windows and the floor was dirt or loose boards on dirt.

There was a song—a western ballad – called "Little Old Sod Shanty on My Claim" which described the claim shack: "...the hinges are of leather...and the windows have no glass...and the board roof lets the howlin' blizzard in...." It was an accurate description.

Accounts have been told of some such buildings being built with wheels, so a settler could declare that there was a dwelling on his land and the building might then be pulled over onto the claim of a neighbor who could then also swear that there was a dwelling on his land! Evidently, officials were not too meticulous in checking as to how long a dwelling remained on site. Some claim shacks became the first unit of a dwelling that was improved and to which additions were made over a number of years. There are farmhouses today which were built around a claim shack, which is now incorporated into a modern home.

Beginning efforts to improve the claim shack would have included covering the walls inside, some of which were papered with newspapers, which helped to keep out the cold winter.

My grandfather's family lived in such a house on the Frank Snyder place, on Rock Creek, southwest of Vilas, which had been made out of two claim shacks which had been moved together to provide more room and which had gradually been improved over the years.

The years immediately before World War I were good years for the village of Vilas. The Vilas <u>Venture</u> (one of three newspapers published at different times in the town) described the businesses and activities underway during the months of January through May 1916: new buildings in the process of construction were the Independent Order of Odd Fellows (IOOF) Hall, the Methodist Church, and a new home and out buildings for my grandfather, G. F. Kilian. Active businesses included Bert R. Anderson, a cream buyer for the North American Creamery Company; a corn shelling business operated by Ed Curvo; a café, the Vilas Lunch Room, operated by W. L. "Bumps" Hanson; J. W. Kusak operated the blacksmith shop; Kilian and Danielson Printing Shop (Milo Kilian, my father's brother and his cousin, Harold Danielson); John Hepner's Department Store; Dave H. McCabe, barber shop; F. B. Raymond, dealer in real estate; Mrs. A. L. Scott operated a cream buying station; Chris Larson owned and operated the Vilas Dray and Transfer Line; B. R. Anderson was agent for the Madison Mill and Grain

Company; C. H. Medhaug ran the C. L. Colman Lumber Company; selling lumber and coal; N. W. Larson operated the J. T. Scoggs Elevator, buying grain; A. J. Vind was a cream and produce buyer; Fred Bentley was a cattle dealer; Wid Raymond was a building contractor for all kinds of carpentry and concrete work. Dan Anderson, a colorful pioneer farmer, raised large onions by the truckload and sold them to area merchants.

Both railroads operated brisk schedules, running about six to eight freight and passenger trains daily and published their schedules in the Vilas <u>Venture</u>. Both of the Hepner Stores – William F. "Bill" Hepner and his father, John Hepner – carried large inventories of great variety. Bill Hepner even had an auto sales agency, selling Metz Motor Cars!

Vilas had an orchestra, which held regular practices and gave public performances in the town and in Howard and surrounding communities.

THE LANDMARKS

BILL HEPNER'S STORE

Hepner's General Store, at the west edge of Main Street on the north side, was the center of business activity and the daily social crossroads. The store owner was William F. Hepner – "Bill" – who was assisted by his wife Ethel and occasionally, Lyle Willey and other ladies in town. The store was indeed general – it had about everything that anyone would need and some things one would only want. It sold food, of course, canned goods and dried goods, and vegetables like potatoes and carrots and fruits like apples, oranges, and bananas and concord grapes (in wooden baskets with wire handles) in season. It even had a fresh meats counter with displays of meats, cheeses and other foods that had to be kept cool. There were eggs –lots of eggs—because Hepner's bought eggs from the area farmers who delivered them in wooden crates, with heavy paper dividers between layers, for sale or trade. Mostly, they were for trade; that is, a farmer would bring in ten dozen eggs or whatever number, for which he would receive so many cents a dozen, which he would then use to pay a part or all of the bill for groceries or other goods he bought.

Bread loaves came by train in large wooden boxes from bakeries in Howard or Madison. There were large crates of bananas with bananas still attached to the stalks. These bunches were hung up on a rope from the ceiling and the bananas were broken off the stalk as they were sold. Wooden boxes, crates and kegs were used to ship many different items to the store. All fruits came in wooden crates, as, peaches, from the West Slope in Colorado. Butter came in one pound blocks wrapped in wax paper. Peanuts and other nuts such as walnuts, almonds and pecans came in small barrels.

Hepner's carried a large supply of candy bars and assorted candies. Baby Ruth bars in those times were three times larger than they are today and sold for .05¢! Soda pop was available in limited choice: orange, grape, lemon, cherry and root beer and a new drink called "Coca Cola." Hepner's stocked all the extra goodies needed for the holidays, like Thanksgiving and Christmas. This included tubs of fresh oysters, herring and dried fish, and candles and ornaments.

In the summertime, eggs from the farms had to be "candled" to ensure that they were still fresh. The storekeeper had to take each egg individually and hold it up to a panel with a hole in it with a bright light source behind the hole. The light would shine through the egg and reveal whether or not it had any dark and cloudy spots in it--the mark of a bad or rotten egg which would disqualify it for sale. Summertime brought some hazards to farmers bringing the produce to town for sale, since they were without refrigeration or any effective means for cooling. Some farmers would lower eggs and cream down into a cistern which was cooler than any area above ground.

The store had a variety of clothing for men: bib overalls, jackets, mittens, work gloves, high-buckle overshoes and rubber boots, chambray shirts, woolen long-john underwear and socks. For women, there were hats and dresses, stockings and shoes. Often, out of financial necessity, women would sew much of the family clothing and other household articles. The store sold bolts of cloth, and varied threads, pins, needles, buttons and patterns, scissors and other items needed by the home seamstress. Nearly every home had a sewing machine which was operated by a foot treadle.

There was a large inventory of hardware items: glass jars for canning food; kitchen wares – pots, pans, knives, dishes and table wares; nails and bolts by the keg; horse collars and leather for straps and buckles and snaps and other harness hardware. There were lamps—kerosene, and the modern mantle lamps which gave a much brighter light – and kerosene lanterns for use in the barns and outdoor sheds. There were pocket knives and fishing tackle and bamboo fishing poles. There were many other things to qualify the place as a true general store.

The building itself was a white, wooden two-story, false front of the type common in the prairie villages all across Dakota. There were large plate glass "store windows" in front, facing the street. An unusual feature in front of the store was a gasoline pump for autos. When an auto pulled up for gas, someone from the store would come out and pump gasoline from an underground tank up into a glass cylinder, using a hand lever on the side of the gas pump. The glass cylinder was marked off in graduations of one gallon each. The gas would flow down by gravity into the auto's tank. One had to watch the glass cylinder to know how much gas had flown into the car.

Kerosene for lamps and stoves and other purposes could be bought by bringing a metal can, usually five gallon, into the store and it would be filled from a tank in the back of the store building.

So, in Vilas, almost everything that was "store-bought" came from Hepner's. Bill Hepner even operated the lumber yard and coal yard down near the Milwaukee railroad depot, at one time. There was a coal yard from which one could buy coal (shipped in by the railroads) by the wagon load to haul home and dump down a chute into a coal bin in the basement of a house. The coal itself was of some variety – the hard coal (anthracite) came generally from the East in Pennsylvania or Illinois or Ohio. Soft coals like lignite were probably from open strip mines in western Dakotas, Wyoming, or Montana.

Hepner's was also the site of the U.S. Post Office for Vilas and thus, Hepner or his wife was listed as the official postmaster. Here everyone came for their mail, for there was no delivery service in town or in rural areas. Here came the letters from relatives, magazines and packages of wonders ordered from far-away mail order houses, plants and seeds from nursery companies and everything else that traveled by mail. Here one bought stamps (.03¢ for letters and a penny for a postcard). Here, one could buy a mail order and send money wherever.

For a number of years, there were two Hepner Stores in Vilas. Bill Hepner's father, John, opened a store in 1911 and was still operating into the late 1930's. John's store was devoted mainly to dry goods, clothing and hardwares.

John was a true pioneer, having come to the area from Wisconsin in 1882. He endured the Blizzard of '88 and other privations of the time before opening his Vilas store. He and his wife, a native of Denmark, had 14 children. They were honored on their 50th wedding anniversary by a large crowd at the IOOF Hall in July, 1936.

FRANK WYNN'S POOL HALL

On the north side of Main Street, the first place of business east of Bill Hepner's store was Frank Wynn's Pool Hall. It was an old white wooden building with a false front, a classic example of the prairie village façade model.

There were high ceilings of pressed metal sheets and big sunny windows facing the street. The wooden chairs around the walls and at the card tables were brownish wood, shiny from long polishing by hands and pants bottoms. There were a few "ice cream" chairs with steel hooped backs. The floors were unfinished wooden boards, worn from thousands of feet over many years. In the summer, the battered screen door kept most of the sleepy, buzzy flies out in the street.

Old Frank sold tobacco and a few items that could be eaten: crackers, candy bars and gum. In those days, there were no bags of chips and crunchies of great variety or any meat jerkies or the dozens of other items now available in such a place. There were no microwave sandwiches. Plastic bags had not yet been invented. It was a much more simple, austere world.

The building may well have had earlier occupants than Frank Wynn, but it was an important place because it was where one could get ice cream! For old men who were past their working years, or nearly so, there were two pool tables and several card tables. It was pretty much a male resort – girls and women only came there to seek out men with a message for them. So, old men played cards, mainly whist. Younger men played pool. Kids came in with nickels to buy ice cream cones. The ice cream was kept in large tubs set down in a counter cooler. Each tub held several gallons and there were a number of flavors: vanilla, chocolate, strawberry, cherry-nut, caramel, blueberry and perhaps others from time to time.

As a boy of five or six, I was a lucky kid to be in Vilas at that time because I was the only little boy of that age. As such, I was a kind of adopted kid for many of the older men in the town. If they were to meet me on the street or at some event, they would very often give me a nickel and send me to the Pool Hall for a cone. Even more wonderful: when old Frank Wynn was emptying out one or more tubs of ice cream to replace them with fresh, new full ones, he would give me a spoon and it was my job to clean out the remaining bits of ice cream in the tubs!

Some of the old card players were regulars, and came every day to sit around the pool hall waiting for others to come, to make up a "game." Once a game began, it might continue all of an afternoon until supper time, with the players smoking cigars and berating the cards they were dealt at every hand. And, they would exchange news and opinion of the things that were whispered about in the community.

The younger pool players smoked cigarettes, and made a great business of racking up the pool balls, of chalking their cues and of measuring the angles of their shots with what they hoped would appear as a practiced eye. Their conversation was generally confined to the dances they had recently attended and the comparative merits of the young women of the area around. Conversations about sporting events were mostly confined to local and national baseball. Professional sports as an industry did not yet exist. Nor were there organized sports programs for kids.

These young men worked as laborers – as workers on farms, or on construction jobs or perhaps in a grain elevator or stockyard. There were no other jobs, for there were no factories or mills or offices or any of the professional and technical jobs now commonly available. And, few of these men went to college or to any training beyond high school. It was considered an attainment to graduate from high school, upon which one went to work in the community.

Frank Wynn seemed to be a very old man. Kids called him "Old Dinty" Wynn. Where the "Dinty" came from is uncertain. He was a kind of frail old fellow, suited for nothing more vigorous than presiding as he did over the card players, the young pool sharks, and still younger ice cream eaters.

Men who hung around pool halls in those days were often held in low regard, unless they were really too old to work. Terms like "pool hall loafer and bum" were often used in derision to indicate social standing or reputation. But, Dinty's Pool Hall wasn't really a low resort and by contrast to many such places, was quite open and airy and sunny and wholesome – or so it seemed to me.

THE IOOF HALL

On the south side of Main Street, across from Frank Wynn's Pool Hall, was the Odd Fellows Hall – The Independent Order of Odd Fellows – a fraternal lodge which was the social center of the town. Any event requiring a large public room or gathering place was held in the "Hall." It was built by the lodge for their meetings and for their women's auxiliary called the Rebekahs. Nearly every family in the area around Vilas belonged to the lodge, in order to be seen as sociable persons and to allow them to participate in many of the activities there.

The Hall was built in 1916, of unusual design. It was a two story wooden frame building seated on a lower story of concrete, which had walls two feet below ground and six feet above ground. The lower floor measured 50 x 50 feet and contained a dining room, kitchen, reception area, club room, office and furnace room. The upper or main floor was a 30 x 50 foot room for public events, and with reception and preparation rooms. It had impressed metal "tin steel" ceiling panels and a floor of hard maple wood. The IOOF Lodge

NO. 96 and the Crocus Chapter of the Rebekah Lodge No. 102 held regular meetings, entertained members of visiting lodges and sponsored many public events there. My grandparents Kilian and their relatives, the Raymond and Danielson families, were all active members and sometime officers of these lodges. The lodges served as a sort of surrogate church for some of their members and their loyalty and attachment was deep and real.

Meetings of the lodge were open only to members as were the women's meetings. There were prescribed rituals and items of apparel, to lend solemnity to the proceedings. But the Odd Fellows sponsored many public social events, principally card parties and dances. The dances were community affairs – anyone could come. In the earlier years, the musicians were an amorphous collection of fiddlers and other family musicians, such as the Merriam Family orchestra and the Merry Maids. They would saw away on waltzes, polkas and other folk tunes. They were seated on a platform about a foot above the dance floor. The musical leader was usually a fiddler who would start the songs, stamping his foot to mark the time and they would labor through, not always completely in time or in tune. There were square dances, with callers to direct the dancers and who were popular in relation to the wit and energy they could bring to calling out the movements.

There were chairs all around the walls for old people who could not dance but who came to watch and to gossip and for older dancers to rest. Couples with young kids and babies would put them to sleep on piles of overcoats and blankets on the floor in the cloakroom and hallways around the dance floor. The kids seemed to sleep peacefully through the entire hub-bub without ill effects. Often, there were refreshments: sandwiches, cakes, jello salads and coffee. Everyone who was physically able to dance did so: old people would limp and hobble – young people would whirl and dash, with great energy. It was a good place for young people to size each other up.

There were other events beside dances and card parties. Some of the larger events of the school were held there, such as speech competitions and declamatory contests with other schools. The Christmas programs were often held there, with a procession of traditional events, replete with Wise Men and Shepherds in bathrobes and towels for turbans. There was a large Christmas tree with a star on top and gifts of brown paper bags full of hard candy and shelled peanuts for all kids. There were plays and recitals and, rarely, traveling speakers, politicians and musicians. A remarkable canvas stage curtain was raised and lowered with light ropes and painted with elaborate advertisements of various businesses, like banks, retail stores, coal dealers, real estate brokers and others on the curtain. It was always exciting when the huge curtain was rolled up and the entertainment was to begin.

In the basement of the hall were tables and a kitchen. Elaborate meals were served on long rectangular tables covered with white cloths. All the food was brought from homes in the community; there was no other option, for there were no food catering services.

The IOOF Hall was the last remaining building of consequence on the Vilas Main Street. Within recent years, the floors of hard maple and the pressed metal ceiling panels and other woodwork were taken out for recycling and the building was razed. Nothing remains today but two spruce trees that remain as solitary sentinels to mark the events of earlier times.

FRANK BERNSTETTER'S GARAGE

Frank Bernstetter's garage was the only place in Vilas – and much of the county – where one could go for car repairs. Cars of that era were mechanically pretty simple. The motors worked on a straight-ahead basis: there were cylinders with pistons to make compression, spark plugs to fire the gasoline vapors, a carburetor to regulate gasoline going into the engine from a gas tank attached somewhere behind the engine. A person who knew how to use wrenches and screw drivers could take a car apart and put it back together and could see directly what needed to be repaired or cleaned.

Frank had a natural affinity for wrenches and greasy machines. He was a man of ordinary stature with mussed up hair who wore old overalls and shirts that were grubby with dust-ingrained grease. Frank worked on stationary engines, too, engines about the size of a large suitcase mounted on a sturdy wooden platform and which were used for many purposes around the farm – to run grinders and mills for grain, to power pumpjacks for water wells and such. And Frank was often asked to fix lots of other small mechanical devices – not just combustion engines. He was a busy man, for he was about the only general fix-it man around.

One's whole impression of the shop, located on the south side of Main Street, a little to the southeast of Hepner's Store, was that Frank and everything in it, tools, boxes, barrels, shelves – everything, was covered with dust-encrusted grease and oil.

Sometimes a farmer whose car had stopped running would hitch up a team of horses to pull the car into Frank's Garage and park it near the door, to be attended to, in order of its arrival.

Everything that happened in that garage was the result of applications of human muscle. There were no hydraulics, no electric hoists or lifts or tools. All tools were muscle-powered. If a car had to be raised up, it was lifted by hand-operated jacks. If a heavy metal engine or assembly had to be raised from its frame, it would be pulled up by a block and tackle of hemp rope.

Replacement parts for cars, as often as not, were taken off of old cars of similar model, parked behind the building or nearby in the town as a resource for that purpose. If a part had to be ordered from a dealer or factory some distance away, it would usually be some days before it would arrive.

For most providers of goods and services in the small towns of that era, cash income was uncertain at best. Often, someone would need car repairs but had no money in hand to pay for it. Frank would have to wait for his money and he had to keep a record of some kind to remember who owed him how much and for what. And, like many small merchants of the time, there were many such bills that never got paid at all: the system was very informal and disorganized.

Gradually, over time, the auto dealers became more involved in the business of repair of their cars. Auto dealers became auto servicers as well and began stocking spare parts and accessories for cars in their local dealerships. They began to hire their own mechanics and tiny garages like Frank's gradually faded away and disappeared entirely.

LAURA FUNKENBUSCH

In a little gray house next to the Odd Fellows Hall lived a little old lady named Laura Funkenbusch. She had two sons, Archie and Daniel (referred to as "Dan'l). An old man named Frank Boomhauer lived with them, for whom she provided board and room. There was a large bay window facing the street which was remarkable in that it had the appearance of lace curtains etched onto the glass – so the curtains never needed washing or pressing!

Boomhauer was regularly, endlessly teased and tormented by Dan'l, who would be chased out of the house and into the street by the enraged Boomhauer, shouting threats of mayhem. Dan'l was a constant trial to Old Boom, as the kids called him. Dan'l wasn't the only burden Old Boom had to bear, for the young kids of the town would sometimes gather near the house and begin chanting "Boom, Boom, Boom..." until the old man would come raging out of the house and the kids would scatter. Some of them would hide up in the branches of the boxelder trees across the street to watch the performance. But, Dan'l was the chief burden that Old Boom carried and it was said that he once proposed to a young man of the town: "I'll give you fifty cents if you'll shoot that Dan'l!" Life was not easy for Mrs. Funkenbusch and she had a quick and violent temper as a result. Old Frank died in 1933.

SWEENEY'S CREAM STATION

Along the south side of Main Street in the center of Vilas was Ross Sweeney's Cream Station. The Cream Station was a small frame false front building where farmers could sell the cream they produced.

Ross lived in a small white house across the street with his wife, Ruth, a son Raleigh and a daughter, Veronica. He took over management of the station in 1928.

Cream produced on area farms was a valuable commodity in the early years. There were a number of cream buyers in Vilas who preceded Ross Sweeney, with stations in several locations.

Every farm had a small herd of cows which the family milked to get milk, cream and the butter and cheese they could make from it. There would always be a surplus of cream which they saved in large metal cans which they could take to town to sell.

On arrival at the station, the farmer would unload one or more cream cans – usually about ten gallons each. The station manager would take a sample of the cream in a test tube and check it for the amount of fat content. The fat content and the weight of the cream would determine how much he would pay the farmer. The cash the farmer received was important, since he had few sources to earn cash income apart from the sale of crops and livestock. The cream money was used to buy food and clothing for the family.

The cream station manager would accumulate a number of cans of cream and he would send them off to the creamery that he represented. Sweeney's cream cans would be hauled to a train depot and shipped. In earlier years, there was a creamery several miles south of Vilas, which closed in 1918. The foundation stones may still be seen today.

At the railroad station, there would be large, four-wheeled flat bottomed carts of cream cans standing on the freight platform, waiting to be loaded on on-coming freight trains.

In those years, cream stations faced real problems: there was no refrigeration. In the high temperatures of summer, the metal cans of cream would sour quickly. A second problem was that concerns for sanitation on the farms were far less than today. It was not unknown for bits of dirt, cow manure and flies to be found in the cans of cream. In the hot days of summer, when temperatures were 90 or 100 or more, some cream would ferment and create gasses which caused the cans to explode – to literally blow up – and scatter sour cream all over the place!

In general, the system worked and both the cream buyer and seller were able to earn a small but important income. Most of the money earned would go to the general store for things the family needed. The sale of cream was an incentive for some farmers to try to build large dairy herds which might require the whole family to help with milking the cows each day. Large herds of cows resulted in building larger barns and silos, to provide feed for the cows.

Majestic Cottonwood trees are everywhere on the prairie and are the de facto State Tree.

Stone ruins of the creamery south of Vilas, which remain today.

THE BLACKSMITH SHOP

Vilas had a blacksmith shop since the town was founded in 1883. In the 1920's and 30's, the blacksmith was still a very important man in the prairie community. Almost all of the farm machines were made of iron – the plows, discs, drags, cultivators, mowers, rakes – everything. When something broke it was the blacksmith who could weld it back together and keep it running.

In Vilas, the blacksmith shop was located in the center of Main Street, on the south side, kittycorner southeast of the hotel. It was a long, weathered, wooden building with a cedar shingle roof (all roofs were cedar shingles or tar paper in those days). It had big garage-type doors facing the street and someone going by could look in and see the fiery forge and the flying sparks.

The blacksmith shop was a wonderful place to watch the smiths and the farmers work miracles with iron and wood. The forge was the chief attraction. It was fired with charcoal and always had a sullen, red glow in its burner. When the blacksmith wanted to heat up a piece of iron for shaping, he would place it over the forge and blow air on the coals until they flared up and glowed with a white heat. When the iron was red-hot, the blacksmith could bend it or hammer it on an anvil with heavy hammers to shape it.

The blacksmith not only could weld broken iron pieces or parts back together, but he could make a new part if he was given a pattern or sketch. Generally, the blacksmith would sharpen tools and machine parts. He would sharpen the plow shares and the shovels for cultivators, He could fashion hard ware for harnesses and wagons and other machines to brace the wooden boxes or reinforce wooden parts of great variety. Blacksmiths could put iron rims on wooden wagon wheels and they could tighten up wooden wheels when the spokes were dried out and the hubs and rims loose.

The Vilas blacksmith shop had a large open iron kettle or tub – big enough to set a wagon wheel down into a dark soup of boiling linseed oil. The oil would soak into the wooden wheel and wood would expand and the iron rim would become tight around the spokes. When fished out of cooking oil the wheel was much heavier and solid as a rock, ready for many miles of rolling behind the horses.

Wheels of great variety were boiled in the oil of this vat – buggy wheels, wheels with narrow and wide iron rims – nearly any wooden wheel from any vehicle could be made sound again by this process.

Linseed oil was understood by nearly everyone as the most useful preservative for wood that existed. The oil was applied to the wooden parts of all kinds of machines – threshers, corn shellers, wagon boxes, hay buckers or whatever. The oil would soak in and vanish quickly into dry wood and so new coats were brushed on until the wood could absorb no more.

The oil would form a layer on the surface of the wood that would protect it from water and other natural erosion. Linseed oil was the base of most paints used on homes and farm buildings. It was used by glaziers to mix with a soft, modeling-clay-like substance called putty to hold panes of window glass in their frames. It could be used to paint the surface of metal to inhibit rust. It was thinned with pine turpentine as a polish and finish for fine cabinet wood and woodwork, within homes. No home was without a supply of linseed oil in those early times.

Now, it is largely forgotten and unknown even though it can still perform its wonders in the preservation of wood. Now people pay absurd prices for many products offered to preserve wood which are essentially worthless. Linseed oil is fairly expensive now because it is so seldom used but it is still available in paint and hardware stores.

Watching the blacksmith swing those big hammers and watching the sparks fly from the red hot iron was fascinating. The place was a mixture of many exotic smells, too – the smoke from the forge, and the hot metal and old leather all blended together to make a distinctive blacksmith shop smell.

Horseshoeing was also a feature of many village shops. The blacksmith may well have made the iron horse shoes to begin with – and in earlier times, he would have made ox shoes and mule shoes as well. The horseshoes were of many different sizes and a stock of these was kept on hand to fit the needs of incoming horses. The farrier had to know how to fit the shoe on the animals and to nail it into place, and to trim the hooves as needed. Old worn out horseshoes were replaced with new ones and the old ones might turn up in the horseshoe pitching pits in the villager's backyard. Many old, worn horseshoes were thrown into a pile to be recycled for many other purposes: they were nailed up on the studs of walls of barns everywhere to use as hooks to hang the leather harnesses, or in other farm buildings as hooks for pails, lanterns, coils of rope or most anything. Old horseshoes were nailed over the entrances to many farm homes and buildings as a sign of good luck. It is uncertain how this custom arose, but it was wide-spread.

There were always piles of scrap iron around a blacksmith shop which served as a stock pile for pieces of iron straps or rods or angle irons or other shapes, to use in making repairs on machinery or in building entirely new inventions and devices according to the customer's order. In such piles one might find parts of all the machines that were in common use in those days and the resourceful blacksmith could create inventive, original solutions to practical problems.

There were many iron items that were made routinely in such shops, such as meat hooks for the smoke house, hay hooks for pulling bundles or bales of hay around, picket pins

The Sweeney's Cream Station. Frank Wynn's Pool Hall.

The Colman Lumber Yard near the Milwaukee Depot.

to drive into the ground to attach the tether rope of animals staked out to graze. There were hinges and hooks and locks for farm and outbuildings and fence gates. There were even wheels and axles for small carts and dollys used to haul heavy items around the farm yard. Almost anything made of iron that was useful around the farm or country home could be and was made in the blacksmith shop.

Now, there is no remaining sign that the blacksmith shop ever existed. Probably archaeologists would find a great variety of iron items buried in the dirt at that site, but today the building is gone, the boxelders are gone and nothing remains on the ground to tell the tale.

THE GEHRING HOTEL

The Gehring Hotel was located on the northwest corner of the intersection of Main Street and East Avenue, east of the post office. A two story, frame building, it was one of the most imposing buildings on the street. It would have been difficult to miss for traveling men coming from either of the train depots. It enjoyed a brisk business for some years. The proprietor was assisted by young women maids. Room rent was $1.40 a night.

Proprietor of the hotel was a man named Gottleib Gehring, a German with a distinct accent and with peculiar patterns of reasoning. His hotel was frequented mainly by traveling salesmen who would come into town on the railroads. He kept a small dining area where breakfasts were served. It was a source of some amusement to the local gossips that Gottleib always kept one table with a bowl of oranges in the center. When guests came to pay their bill, Gottleib would always ask them, "Did you sit at the table with the oranges on?" If they did, he would charge them twenty-five cents ex-

The Commercial Hotel (above), the Gehring Hotel (left) and the Independent Order of Odd Fellows Hall (below) were among the largest buildings in Vilas.

tra, for if they did not eat any oranges, they could have done so!

During the summer season, the outside walls, and screens and windows were always covered with boxelder bugs in great profusion, because of the very large old boxelder trees that stood along the street.

The small hotels of the pioneer villages provided an austere lodging. Most had fewer than a dozen rooms. The rooms were furnished with an iron bedstead, a table and chair and a lamp – in later years, a single electric bulb hung from the ceiling by its cord. There were wash basins of crockery or tin and a water pitcher, as well as a chamber pot. There were no closets for clothing, only wall hooks or an iron rod or dowel held up at either end. Lace curtains hung at the single window.

There was a common room or dining area on the main floor where guests could congregate, near the registration desk. There were usually a few well-worn books or magazines. If food was served, there would be one menu for all at a given meal.

The smallest and most simple of these hotels were among the first casualties when improved roads and better cars allowed people to travel farther for better service.

THE LIVERY BARN

One business which is largely unknown to many people today was the livery barn. The Vilas Livery Barn was located on the south side of Main Street about two blocks southwest of the Northwestern Depot. Vilas' first livery man was Stephan A. Russell, a pioneer who arrived early and settled north of Vilas in 1881. Briefly put, a livery barn was a "motel" for horses and, sometimes, mules – that were visitors or transients in town and had to have a place to stay while their masters were about some local business. Such a barn would have a number of stalls, with mangers and oats boxes, in which horses could be tied up or penned in during their stay. Usually, like a barn on a farmstead, there was a hay mow in the second story to store the prairie hay to feed the visitors. There was space outside and sometimes inside the barn where buggies or wagons could be parked as well.

Vilas' livery barn was a barn of gray weathered wood with a fairly low ridgepole on the shingled roof. There was a hay door in the front of the hay mow, facing main street.

In earlier times, the livery barn served as a taxi stand for travelers who got off the trains and had to travel locally. They could go to the barn and rent a horse or team and wagon or buggy for a specific time and fee. The barn was also a place where students who came to the school could leave their horses and buggy, if any, through the day while they were in classes and return in the late afternoon for the journey of several miles home.

The proprietor of the livery barn owned some horses which he kept there both for rent and to pull the delivery or freight wagon that he might also have for rent, to haul freight from the railroad depots or between other parties in the community. Some horses were boarded at the barn for extended periods, depending on the convenience of their owners.

Students who attended school in Vilas and who might come every day in a light "democrat" wagon to the livery barn, left their horses and wagon and walked to the school building which was about a half mile to the northwest. When there was a lot of traffic around, the barn was a great place to come and watch the procession of people and horses, in and out. And, it was fun for kids to play up in the hay mow, if the owner was not too strict.

A traveling salesman who might come to town on one of the trains, would often have several large wooden cases or trunks full of samples of his products to show prospective buyers. He could walk from the train station to the livery barn, strike an agreement with the barn owner for a horse and buggy on which he could load his cases, in order to make the rounds of his visit and to deliver the trunks back to the railroad depot when he was ready to leave town.

Shelter for the animals was especially important during the heavy days of winter, to provide relief from the winds and blowing snow and a place with a dry stall and dry feed.

So, before the age of the automobile, the livery barn was the center of a lot of activity and performed a real service to the prairie people. The Vilas Livery Barn was torn down in 1937.

THE RAYMOND LAND OFFICE

The Raymond Land Office was located on the south side of Main Street, adjoining the livery barn. It was a small, wooden frame building, one story, with slanted roof behind the ubiquitous false front. It was the office of Farmer B. Raymond, my great uncle, brother of my grandmother, Emma Kilian. Farmer came to Vilas on or before 1900; how he learned of the town or when he first came is unknown. He was operating a real estate office in Aurora, Illinois in 1895. He came from the Raymond family seat in Winslow, Illinois near the Wisconsin line.

F.B. Raymond was an ideal personality to serve as a real estate promoter. He thought and talked expansively, with an air of assurance and authority. He could paint spellbinding verbal pictures of the grand things the future held. He was the center of attention in any small gathering. He advertised himself as "F. B. Raymond – the Land Man" in the small newspapers in the area. His name was painted in large letters on the outside of his office building. He was a natural extrovert and politician.

Uncle Farmer was responsible for persuading my grandparents Kilian and other families to move to Vilas from Illinois. He had dreams of making a great fortune in the land business in Dakota. He talked Grandmother Kilian into lending him all the money in her sizable legacy and he attracted other investors. He began buying old homesteads and deserted farms in north central South Dakota. At one time, in association with "Hawkeye Mike" Michel and others, he had assembled one of the largest ranches that ever existed in that area. But as is often the case, wild ambition ends in sorrow and they lost it all. They had become land rich and cash poor and could not even pay the taxes on their holdings in the end. So, Grandma and the others lost it all, too.

In the course of his travels, Uncle Farmer attended the meetings and conventions of the fraternal order called the Independent Order of Odd Fellows. He impressed many of the lodge leaders that he met around the nation and he rose in influence until he was finally elected Grand Master of the Order, for the whole nation, with offices in Chicago.

The Vilas Odd Fellows maintained a cemetery for their members and families a mile north of Vilas on a small knoll, bordered by thorny locust trees and with a huge cluster of lilacs in the center.

The funeral conducted there for Farmer Raymond was an impressive event. He was the chief official of the national organization and the funeral was the occasion for a remarkable display of pageantry. There were large striped tents, banners and flags and colorfully uniformed officials, covered with braid and ornaments, who moved about and conducted the service with great ceremony and pomp. It was a memorable event. Farmer Raymond's tombstone remains today as the dominant feature of the neglected cemetery.

After years of standing empty and abandoned on Main Street, the Raymond Land Office was moved to the DeHaven Stockyards to serve as an office. Finally, when the stockyards closed, the office was torn down and the wood recycled for other purposes in the community.

DEHAVEN'S STOCKYARDS

Just east of the Northwestern Railroad tracks, on the east side of Vilas were the stockyards, owned by Tom DeHaven. Farmers in a radius around the town brought their cattle for sale, to be shipped off to a meatpacker in cattle cars on the Northwestern Railroad. Cattle cars were designed much in the same way as the large semi stock trucks are today, with slots and holes and perforations along the side for air to flow in and out, with a tight roof overhead for rainy or wet weather.

The cattle coming to the yards were sometimes driven there by men on foot or horseback. They came from small herds, most of whom were a mixed lot. Registered cattle existed but were rare. Most of the cattle were a mixed and mongrel lot, with all colors: red roan, blue roan, white, red and black and many variations of spots. The preference was for Holsteins, to produce milk and cream for family use and for sale.

DeHaven, along with my grandfather and others had moved to Vilas from Northern Illinois, in pursuit of opportunities in "the West." Tom DeHaven was a large man with an imposing personal presence, and a forceful personality. He was more given to quick decisive action than to reflection. He wore a large cattleman's felt hat and a vest and smoked cigars as did many of the men of that era.

The yards were divided into holding pens of varied sizes, adjoining some native grass pasture. Here the cattle were sorted into lots and shipments for rail transport. There was a complex system of alleyways and chutes connecting the various pens so that the cattle could be moved about to suit varied purposes.

Tom DeHaven owned what the villagers called a "bull wagon," which was used to go out to the farms to pick up large, fierce or unruly bulls to haul them to the yards. The wagon was built of heavy dimension lumber, with sides close together to insure the bull had little room to slam around, and with a top to keep it from rearing up and breaking out. It was like a heavy jail cell on wooden wagon wheels, with the driver seated in the front, as on a stagecoach, and pulled by two horses. It was a common sight to see the bull wagon slowly plodding along a township road headed for Vilas with a heavy and resentful old bull inside. Once arrived at the stockyard, he would be confined in a pen not unlike the wagon – heavy, high sided fences to keep him in check.

The stockyards, one of the largest business enterprises in the town, required a number of sturdy men to handle the cattle – to feed and water them and haul in hay and straw, to drive and sort them, clean the pens and finally to herd them through the alleys and up the chute into the railroad cars for shipment. Among the long-time employees was Bill Wriggs, who lived in a little gray house directly across the street from Bill Hepner's Store. Two Wriggs kids, Leslie, nicknamed "Moose" because he was unusually large and action-oriented, and a girl, Vernetta, attended the Vilas school.

When the yards were full of cattle, there was a constant bellowing and mooing, with occasional shrill trumpets from the large old pasture bulls. Like people, some cattle had peculiar and individual voices and one could learn to attach the sound to the animal.

DeHaven was a careful manager and became quite prosperous as a cattle buyer, and over time invested in farms around the county. He was a man of affairs and was generally looked to for leadership in the town. What Tom thought had an influence on what less forceful citizens thought. He lived in one of the finer homes on a hill overlooking the stockyards with his wife, Tillie, and young son, Freddie.

The stockyards was a product of its time, serving the needs of that time and like much of the activity of that era, faded way, as a result of changes in how people farmed, how they traveled and moved goods around and of technical changes of great variety. Like the horse and buggy, it was no longer needed anymore. Better roads and bigger trucks made shipping to markets like Sioux Falls a more attractive option. The decline of the railroads spelled the end. Finally, new technology and transportation changed that facet of village life, as it did everything else.

HEAR THE TRAIN BLOW...

The railroads were the major factor in the settlement of the town of Vilas and most of the small towns in eastern South Dakota. While there had been explorers and travelers and settlers in the area before the coming of the railroads, railroads hauled in the people, equipment and livestock that created rural communities.

Vilas itself was the product of the Western Town Lot Company, an agency that followed the railroads. Their employees laid out the town and measured off the lots to be sold. The town was named in honor of Col. W. F. Vilas, a prominent Territory attorney and Wisconsin senator, who became the postmaster general of the United States.

The location of the town sites along the railroads was determined by how far a rural family would normally be willing to travel from their home to buy supplies and to trade eggs, cream and other farm produce. Thus, a new town was established about every five to eight miles along the railroad route. In Miner County, that accounted for Howard,

Vilas, Roswell, and Fedora, all in a row along the Chicago, Milwaukee, St. Paul and Pacific Railroad, and Carthage, Argonne and Canova, along the Northwestern Railroad. Vilas was founded in 1883.

Vilas had two railroads, the Milwaukee, running east and west and the Chicago and Northwestern, running from the northwest to the southeast. The two intersected in the town of Vilas. When the advance agents were buying rights-of-way to build the Northwestern, it was in the name of the Dakota Central Railroad, which was sold to the Chicago and Northwestern Railroad, the name by which it was called when it built through Vilas in 1883.

Both of these railroads had their own depots, side tracks and local agents. Each had freight platforms and storage sheds at the depots and hand trucks to load and unload the train cars. The Northwestern had a coal supply station and a large water tower. A section of the depot was walled off and furnished with a ticket window, heavy wooden benches and wrought-iron frames and a large iron stove to accommodate passengers, coming and going. The station agent served as the ticket-seller. There was a stack of worn newspapers left by passengers traveling through, which were studied idly by locals lounging in the waiting room between trains.

The presence of the two railroads elevated Vilas to serve as a center for commercial exchange in the county: there were great piles of mail sacks and boxes and crates of freight of every description to be moved about. In those days, everything traveled by rail, for there were no trucks. Highways and trucking systems as we know them today did not exist. Nor were there busses for public transportation. If man or package traveled, it was by rail. The freight trains carried a great deal more than mail and packages. They hauled away from Vilas tons of grain from the bulging grain elevators and hundreds of cattle from the crowded stockyards, all to be processed in distant cities and to make room for more, coming off of the area farms.

Vilas had a number of people whose work was the transfer of all of this material on and off and between trains. Some handled the U. S. mail; some handled only freight and some kept the railroad tracks in good repair.

Between the two railroads, there were as many as 20 trains a day passing through Vilas. During the harvest seasons, there were very long freight trains hauling grain from many rural elevators to the mills and markets to the east and south. These trains sometimes had 100 cars or more, stretching a mile long, pulled by two or three large steam locomotives.

The passenger trains carrying people and mail were much shorter with from five to a dozen cars. The passenger cars were generally well furnished with heavy, plush cushioned seats and tiny wash rooms at the end of each car. These cars were supervised by a conductor, who would take tickets on boarding, helped the infirm to get seated and generally kept order. Only large passenger trains had a dining car.

Other staff aboard the train were an engineer; one or more firemen, who shoveled coal into the fireboxes to heat the steam boilers that drove the engine; one or more brakemen, who were responsible for the hook-up of the cars, for signaling at depots along the way, making switches to side tracks and monitoring the condition of the wheels and couplings between the cars. These men usually rode in the caboose, the last car on the train. Other incidental workers aboard might be cooks and waiters in the dining cars, if any, postal workers in the mail cars, to sort and sack up mail for transfer while en route and stewards in the sleeping cars.

Critical to the railroad operation were the section crews, who worked to keep the road beds – the rails and cross ties – in good repair. These men were called Section Workers because they cared for a section or specified distance of track,

Above: The Northwestern Railroad Depot, the water tower and the west edge of the stockyards.

Left and Below: Two views of the Milwaukee Railroad Depot.

Above: An early passenger train derailed at Vilas.

Left: The Northwestern water tower provided water for train engines.

Below: Passengers wait amid cream cans and freight.

38

from their base of operation. Vilas had a number of section workers who would go out from the town to repair broken rails or joints, replace old worn wooden ties or timbers holding up a tressle over a creek bed or to replace loose spikes or whatever needed attention. They would travel down the track on what were called "hand cars." These were small four-wheeled carts, built to fit and run along the rails of the track. Early models of these cars were literally hand-cars, for they were moved forward by two men pumping up and down on a teeter-totter-like set of handles, connected to gears to turn the wheels of the car. Later models were powered by engines.

Section men had heavy work, lifting long iron rails, large wooden ties, swinging sledge hammers to drive the thick iron spikes into the ties to hold the rails in place. Section workers would go out with their lunch pails and be gone all day, returning at sundown.

The arrival of a train at a depot was always an occasion for bustling activity. Hand-drawn freight carts with four wooden iron-rimmed wheels were lined up along the edge of the freight platform. They were loaded with mail sacks, boxes, crates, and barrels and cream cans. The train moved slowly to a stop at the platform, with much hissing of steam and clanging of metal couplings.

The train engine would still be softly choo-chooing and snuffing and snorting, from steam leaks and water in the boiler. The passengers were lined up along the platform with their suitcases and baggage, ready to board, waiting for passengers getting off the train to clear the way. The train crews would swing down off the cars. Piles of freight and mail were unloaded and new loads put aboard. The station master moved quickly about, with a sheaf of papers in hand. When all the cars had been unloaded and reloaded with cargo and people, the brakeman waved his arm to the engineer, who started a measured, heavy chug-chug, slowly gaining

Handcars of varied design were used by crews to keep railroad tracks in repair. They were literally hand powered; men rode them to work.

speed as the train rolled down the track and away, out into the world.

Back at the depot, the station master was busy on the telegraph key, tapping out messages in Morse Code to go down the telegraph line to the train's next stops. The freight which had been unloaded onto the platform carts had to be hauled and transferred to the other railroad, to local businesses, to the post office or to a freight room, where it would await pickup by individuals. In a half hour or so, peace would reign again, awaiting the next arrival. The smells that hovered over a freight platform were a unique mixture of coal smoke and steam from the engines, creosote from the rail ties and the wooden timbers of the platform. The special and peculiar smells that came from the freight shipments, which might vary enormously, including crates of banana or other fruits, drums of petroleum, big boxes of bread loaves and other goods of great variety.

The trains didn't stop at sundown. Large freights continued through, into the night, loaded with grain or other commodities. For villagers and farm families snug in their beds at night, there was a kind of comfort and reassurance to hear the distant, lonesome whistle of the steam locomotive clickety-clicking through the night. There is an American folk song which was modified to capture something of the mood created by these night trains: "Down in the valley...the valley so low...late in the evening...hear the train blow!"

One of the cogs in the machine that made the wheels of the railroad economy turn in Vilas was Chris Larsen and his mail truck. Chris was an old, white haired native of Denmark who often wore a small dark cap with a stiff leather bill such as are worn by sea captains in North Europe. He was slight of build but strong in dignity and personal demeanor. His truck was a model T Ford with heavy brass headlights which he would polish with a soft cloth until they shown like the sun.

Chris' job was hauling mail sacks – the large bags of heavy gray canvas full of mail – between the depots of the two railroads – to the Milwaukee, running east and west and to the Northwestern, running roughly north and south. All mail traveled by train. Since the railroad crossed in Vilas, mail came and left there from all directions, following the transfer from one railroad to the next. Some small fraction of the mail went to the Vilas Post Office, for local distribution.

Trains had mail cars, with postal employees on them, busily sorting mail as they rolled down the track, to be dropped off at train stops and to go on to wherever.

Chris Larsen took his job very seriously. He sat up very straight behind his steering wheel, with the air of a person on a mission. Because there were many trains each day on both railroads, Chris made many trips between them and to the Vilas Post Office, located about halfway between them. It was an interesting job to have in a small town: one was part of a larger pattern of happenings, tied to the outside world of affairs. It was an important job, too, linked to the U. S. Postal Service, which was held in much higher public esteem then, than in more recent times.

I was a fortunate little kid of five or six years old when during warm summer days, I was allowed to sit beside Chris in the front seat of the Model T truck and serve as his "assistant!" I saw many things riding back and forth and at the depots, waiting for trains to come and go, watching people and freight move on and off the trains, watching the train crews – brakemen, conductors, engineers, depot agents – and the passengers – a little different every time. I saw things many folks never got to see and I learned how the system all fit together.

In support of the Chicago, Northwestern Railroad's operations in Vilas was a large water tower, located on a sidetrack, north of their depot on Main Street. The tower was a huge tank, built of wooden staves, like an oversized barrel.

Iron bands around it, top and bottom, kept the water swollen staves tight, and prevented leaks of any consequence.

Water was pumped into the tank from a nearby well. The purpose of the tank was to provide water to add to the boilers of the steam locomotives that pulled the trains. The hot coal fires that heated the boilers to make the steam, would boil the water away and it had to be restored to keep the engine moving. Engines would pull up to the tower and take on water from a large hose, rather like a modern gas station.

The tower was 40 to 50 feet high, supported by huge square wooden timbers, as legs, below. The pillars were probably 18 inches square and were braced in all directions. The entire tower was painted with a dark brownish-purple lead paint, which dried into a flexible covering almost like thin leather. The bottoms of the pillars rested on huge blocks of buff-colored limestone. The entire area underneath the tower was covered with a crunchy bed of cinders from the fireboxes of the locomotives.

A remarkable feature of the water tower pillars were the countless initials, symbols and artistic efforts that were carved with pocket knives into the heavy paint on the pillars. These were initials and names of men from places and distant cities that were only names in Vilas: from Kansas and Ohio and Colorado and Arkansas and everywhere in the nation. They were carved by the hobos who dropped off the trains, streamed through Vilas by the dozens – sometimes by the hundreds – every week in the warm months of the 1930's. Most of them were on a hopeless search for work, for a way to earn money to send home to the family they had left behind. Some were simply vagrants and drifters – adventurers out to see the world or to "travel on..." compulsively, from one town to the next county, to the next state.

In 1920's, there was a popular ballad called "The Big Rock Candy Mountains," which described the ideal wonderland that all hobos presumably sought. In part, the lyrics said

"In the Big Rock Candy Mountains, there's a land that's fair and bright...the handouts grow on bushes and you sleep out every night...where the boxcars all are empty and the sun shines every day... on the birds and the bees and the cigarette trees...by the lemonade springs where the bluebird sings...in the Big Rock Candy Mountains."

In the height of the Great Depression in the 1930's, there were sometimes a hundred or more hobos riding the box cars on a single train.

If the box cars were loaded with freight and the doors were closed, the hobos rode on the tops of the cars. If the cars were empty, they sat in the open doorways. When trains stopped in Vilas, many hobos got off, to stretch their legs and look around town. There were no railroad police in those days to keep these free-riders off the cars, for it would have been a fruitless effort anyway; everyone knew why they were there.

Once off the train, the hobos fanned out over the town, knocking on doors and asking for food. The housewives were familiar with the process. The man at the door was given bread or a sandwich, perhaps some cold meat, canned food or coffee or whatever was at hand. Rarely were they ever refused, for the women were generous people who knew that the hobos were in need and they felt obligated to share. A remarkable feature of the time was the general attitude of openness and trust with which these exchanges were carried out. I never heard of a single instance of theft, assault or other misbehavior on the part of the traveling men. They were courteous and considerate of others.

The hobos established a "jungle" along the railroad tracks north of the water tower, down in a large clump of willows. Here they brought the food they had collected and heated it over a bonfire of willow sticks. They made coffee in large, one–gallon tin cans, seated on rocks at the edge of the fire. Throughout the summer, there was always coffee left behind by the fire for the next group from the next train that would follow along shortly.

Being curious, other boys and I would go down to the jungle and poke around and perhaps add some sticks to the fire to keep it alive. Occasionally, there would be one or more hobos there and we would visit with them. It never occurred to us to be frightened by these unkempt travelers. Such an exchange would be unthinkable today, because of the changes that have taken place in the society over the years since that time.

When I grew older, going into high school, trains came to have a new meaning for me. The year I was to enter high school in Vilas the decision was made to close the school; all high school students would have to go to Howard, four miles east. I had no car and I was too young to drive, anyway, though there were no driver's licenses or tests, in those days. There was an option: I could ride the Milwaukee train, going east to Howard in the morning and west in the late afternoon to Vilas. There were enough trains running in those days to allow one to commute! The fair was .10¢ each way, but quite often I would be the only passenger. The conductor would open the door of the car, look in, see me and turn way and leave. So, in a tiny way, the Milwaukee Railroad financed a part of my education!

As high school kids, we used the Milwaukee for recreation in the summer as well. On a few occasions, Jim Cooley, son of the Northwestern depot agent, and I would crawl into an empty box car and go for a ride, simply for something to do. We could ride to the east as far as Madison or Egan – about 50 miles – and come back on a west-bound train. We could do this in an afternoon and in some small measure, it added to our education. We would sit in the open door of the box car, with our legs hanging out and watch the world go by, listening to the clickety-click of the big iron wheels on the rails. The noise and the smell of the engine smoke and the swaying of the cars had a certain appeal. One could better understand the freedom that means of travel offered to the vagabond hobo, who traveled simply for the sake of it. I don't think we ever told our parents about those trips, but then, they never asked us!

The prairie railroads, like the prairie towns and an entire way of life have been gradually fading away since the First World War. Now, not even the road beds of the railroad tracks are visible in the tall grass that grows over them, around Vilas. All this has been a casualty of time and the erosion of change.

THE TOWN SITE WAR

The new little town of Vilas had a difficult beginning in 1883. The Chicago, Milwaukee, St. Paul and Pacific Railroad had built west to Vilas and on west to Roswell. The Chicago and Northwestern Railroad was building south toward the center of Miner County. The leadership in Howard tried to get the railroad to move its track east from the Vilas right of way so that the railroad would run through Howard instead of Vilas. Their efforts were in vain and the tracks were built so that they crossed the Milwaukee tracks at Vilas.

It was assumed that a thriving town would spring up at this important new junction. A company whose purpose was to promote the town site and sell lots moved in. The company, Myers, Kilby and Company, sent an agent, J. A. Murphy, to represent them. Murphy was well aware of the existence of the town of Howard, three and one-half miles to the east, which was already well-established and had a population of 700 people.

There have been undercurrent murmurings for years about the early-day "Courthouse War" between Howard and Vilas. In fact, it was not a courthouse war at all, but rather a turf war, a tempest-in-a-teapot battle which might be called a "town-site war." Howard had been declared the county seat and was already building a courthouse building in 1883.

Mr. Murphy, the representative of Myers, Kilby and Company, proved to be an aggressive competitor. A report was circulated by a Chicago newspaper, the Chicago Inter Ocean, in late April, 1884, that the businesses in Howard were going to be moved to Vilas! This resulted from an interview by the Chicago paper with an attorney in Huron, H. M. Jewett. The rumors were repeated in other area newspapers.

The city fathers in Howard went ballistic. A report had been circulated that the "Dubuque House," a local hotel, was to be moved to Vilas. They confronted the hotel owner, a Mr. Bettinger, who denied that he intended to move. However, there was apparently some basis for the idea, as the Howard city fathers accused the Vilas agent, Murphy, of getting Bettinger drunk and getting his agreement thereby. Bettinger next claimed that the hotel building would move only if he were paid $4,000 for it.

The Howard leadership, to discredit the idea that all the businesses in Howard would be moved to Vilas, drew up a statement which was signed by every businessman in town and many other property owners. The signers stated that they intended to remain in Howard and would do so until Vilas was "a thing of the past!" The entire statement was published in the Howard Farmer on March 28, 1884.

Through March and April, 1884, the Howard Farmer devoted a number of long stories to discredit any rumors about Howard being moved bodily to Vilas. The stories were filled with insults and invectives against Vilas, which the editor accused of being a "paper town" which was being promoted by "unprincipled land boomers."

Howard's disdain for Vilas, a town site only a few months old, was in their description of the place as having "a small store, a saloon and a blacksmith shop and a population of about a dozen people and not even having a post office" and that no lots had as yet been recorded with owners at the office of the Register of Deeds.

Murphy was accused of plying Bettinger with liquor and getting him to agree to a proposition which he would never have accepted if sober. The paper reported that when accused, Murphy was arrogant and defiant and had a "personal encounter" with one of the Howard citizens of the "better class" in which Murphy "got the worst of it."

One of the pioneer settlers in Howard, a Mr. John Charnley, bought the principal business then in Vilas, a boot and shoe factory, and moved it to a site in Howard just north of the Dubuque House.

The <u>Farmer</u> heaped abuse on the Huron newspaper and the Chicago Inter Ocean for being guilty of careless and irresponsible journalism and questioned their motives.

The <u>Farmer</u> editor apparently felt given the disdain and depreciation he had heaped on Vilas, together with the move of the shoe factory, would settle the question of any serious competitive challenge from Vilas. Howard had won the fight because its heart was pure!

The Howard newspaper accounts represented only the Howard side of the story, since Vilas did not yet have a newspaper. Ultimately, three different newspapers were published there, to report Vilas to the world.

The unpleasantness over the incident about moving businesses did little to deter Vilas from developing into the important transportation center of the county and the center for the shipping of goods and produce in and out of the county.

As is often the case, elements of the stories like the above are repeated for years in a community. Even in the 1920's and 1930's, some older people harbored feelings of distrust and reserve for Howard, which they regarded as having cheated them out of a larger place in the sun. And, it had taken on the idea of having been a courthouse fight, which was never the case.

LIFE IN AND AROUND VILAS

THE KILIANS IN VILAS

When Grandfather Kilian and family first arrived in Vilas from Illinois, they lived for a brief time in a little house on the Main Street of Vilas. After a few months, they moved to the Frank Snyder place, southwest of Vilas on Rock Creek. From there, they moved to a farmstead about a mile north and west of Vilas, where father broke the virgin sod with a walking plow. They lived there until they bought a farm on the west edge of Vilas, within the town's platted area. The land they bought was all grass, no buildings and not a single tree. There, they built a house and a set of buildings. My father and his brother, Milo, dug the basement using a horse-drawn fresno (a dirt scraper-bucket resembling the scoop on a modern power shovel). They used spades to square up the walls and corners and threw out the dirt by hand. They hauled the dirt from the basement to fill a low spot in a field south of the house.

My great-uncle, Wid Raymond (Grandma Kilian's brother), was the chief carpenter for the construction of the house, barn and other buildings on the farm. Uncle Wid was a skilled builder and later was one of the contractors who built the tall state capitol building in Lincoln, Nebraska. Uncle Wid got all of his lumber from the Vilas Lumber Yard, a quarter mile east, near the Milwaukee depot. All of the cement work was done by Wynn's of Vilas, including the basement, cistern and all the footings for the buildings. Grandpa Kilian drilled a new 200 foot well and put up a windmill north of the house. I was born in an upstairs bedroom in that house.

A view of Vilas from the southwest side of town.

The Kilian home was on the west edge of town, at the end of Main Street.

On the southeast side of the house facing the driveway, was a large clump of yellow Harison roses. These roses were from the earliest times to be found in the front yard of nearly every home in the area. Settlers bought the plants from mail-order houses because they were among the few available that could withstand the winters of that time. Harrison roses dependably provided an explosion of bright yellow blooms on or near Memorial Day. One may still see these roses today near some old abandoned farm homes, still blooming on schedule in the spring. Harrison roses were among the earliest roses in America, introduced about 1836.

There was large garden just west of the house where Grandma Kilian planted rows of gooseberry and red currant bushes and a big rhubarb patch. Grandpa Kilian was very fond of big onions and he had a large potato patch. There were long rows of green beans and peas which we ate raw right out of the pods.

The small farm was typical of that day: a few cows, horses and pigs, free-ranging chickens around the yard, pigeons in the barn. Barn swallows nested under the eves and robins in the garden bushes. Grandpa and my father had a small business selling medicines and tonics for farm animals. The advantages of village and farm life were combined there.

When I entered school in Vilas, I was regarded as a "town kid" rather than a "farm kid" since our house was technically located in the town of Vilas. But there was little or no distinction between town and country kids in those times; they all lived and thought and behaved in the same ways.

The only real spanking I received from my father was at that house. When I was about four or five years old, I was playing outdoors one day in the late fall and there was a wind blowing from the northwest. I gathered up a pile of dead grama grass from the front lawn and piled it up against the south side of the house, got some stick matches from the kitchen and set fire to it. I was making a bonfire to keep warm! Luckily, someone saw me and what was happening and put out the fire. My father when he heard about it was not amused. He took me out to the granary and with a wooden paddle, pounded my bottom until I was red and stiff. He wanted to impress me that such fires were not approved and I never forgot.

My brother Austin told me that he received a similar spanking after he opened up the hood on grandfather's Overland car, parked in the back yard, and pounded the spark plugs with a claw hammer!

EARLY AMERICANA

Just west of Hepner's Store, the land sloped down quite sharply to a small creek that flowed from the northeast to the southwest; it was probably a branch of Wolf Creek. There was a wooden foot bridge that ran across the creek bed, of gray, weathered wood, with railings on both sides. Our house was on to the west about four or five blocks. One day, when I was about five years old, I had been to Hepner's Store and was running down the walk and across this bridge barefooted, when I jammed a huge wooden sliver into the bottom of my foot. I was carried home by a brawny villager, with me bawling loudly all the way. At home, my mother and grandmother took me in hand and they immediately prepared what was called a "poultice" on my injured foot. The poultice was a mixture of flour, herbs and cream spread on a cloth which was wrapped around my foot. Its purpose was to draw out the sliver. This seems like a silly old wives' tale cure today, but amazingly, in two to three days when the bandage was unwrapped in inspection of the progress, there was the sliver suck in the poultice! It was a wicked looking thing about an inch long, which had been driven deep into my foot. The wound healed promptly and I was soon trotting around barefooted again.

I suspect the knowledge of the poultice came from my grandmother. She grew up on the frontier in northern Illinois of Old American stock. Her ancestors came from Virginia and she was full of hand-me-down lore of the early Appalachian culture. When I was a very little kid, sitting on her lap in an ancient rocking chair she brought with her from Illinois, she told me stories that her parents had told her and that her grandparents had told them and so on. The stories and songs she sang made a deep impression on me. She told of Johnny Appleseed who planted trees across the west. She sang songs like "Go Tell Aunt Rhody that the old Gray Goose is dead." She was a living example of traditional early America. She knew everything about the old methods of home preservation of foods – of canning, smoking, salting, drying and other bits of homemaking wisdom which she learned from her parents.

"SKONKY" SORENSON

Just up the hill from the wooden footbridge lived an old man named Nels Sorenson with his wife. Their small, low house was surrounded by trees and bushes and to the west of it was a very large garden. Among the many things Nels raised were watermelons. Every summer the Vilas kids kept close and appraising eyes on this watermelon patch. For reasons unknown, the kids called old Nels "Skonky" and Skonky's watermelons were widely known to be exceptionally sweet and flavorful. One evening in late summer, the kids decided it was time to strike – the melons would be at their prime. This was known because two boys had already gone in as advance party to test them and had plugged one (cut out a triangular sample) with a pocket jackknife and found it ripe and ready. The kids moved in with stealth and caution and were ready to carry off some prizes when a loud report startled them into realizing that they had been seen, and Skonky was dusting them with rock salt fired from his old shotgun! Skonky had been there before and the kids fled empty handed.

R. M. "RAM COOLEY

The station agent for the Northwestern was R. M. "Ram" Cooley, who lived with his family in quarters within the depot. Ram was a living example of the station agent but he did so with difficulty: he had a wooden leg. The leg was lost in an accident in which he was hit with some heavy timbers and it was painful for him to walk. Doubtless because of the pain, he developed a harsh temper which he would sometimes turn on his wife, a very quiet dutiful lady, and his children. He would sit in his office in the depot with a green visor over his eyes, and elastic bands on his upper arms, tapping away, lickety-split on his telegraph key. The telegraph was central in the operation of the railroad with messages going back and forth between depots and distant offices. And the telegraph was the only way of reaching a local citizen quickly. Messages of death and disaster were sent over the telegraph wire, and for a local person to receive a telegram was an ominous occasion and of wide interest to the gossips of the town.

The Northwestern depot passenger waiting room was something of a social center for the locals who came to watch the trains come and go, as well as to meet or deliver passengers. Like most small town depots, it was furnished with a large iron pot-bellied stove which was kept going with coal from a large bucket, and the fire was tended by those who were present at a given time. It was also a place where one could come and "read the paper" – the daily newspapers brought in on the trains and for many their only contact for news of the larger world.

Locals were fond of recounting the story of an old man of the town who came often to the waiting room to "read the paper." The problem was he was illiterate and could not read at all but did not want to admit it. He was known at times to hold the paper upside down and pose as if he were reading to impress those present!

THE ROCK CREEK STAGE STATION

It was still possible in the 1930's to find the site of an old stage coach station that was located in Rock Creek, southwest of Vilas. Few people now are aware of the existence of that site. My father, Ward V. Kilian played in that station with his little brother, Milo, when the station was still standing in about 1910. The boys lived on what was locally called the Snyder Place, just across the road from the stage station.

Father and his brother spent a lot of time in the old stage station and he remembered it well. He described it carefully to me and I drew a floor plan of the station as it was when he was there. (A sketch of that floorplan is included in this book).

Father said that the road that ran between their house and the stage station had been an old Indian trail that had been in use for many years. He said that they used to watch from the farm yard as bands of Indians with horses would go by their place, going to and fro between the Flandreau area to the east and the Crow Creek reservation west, along the Missouri. The Indians went back and forth to visit relatives. They were members of the Santee, whose ancestors had been shipped to Crow Creek from Minnesota, following the War of the Outbreak in 1862. They had been placed on steamboats and

ROCK CREEK STATION

CYCLONE CELLAR

SHED

STAGE STATION

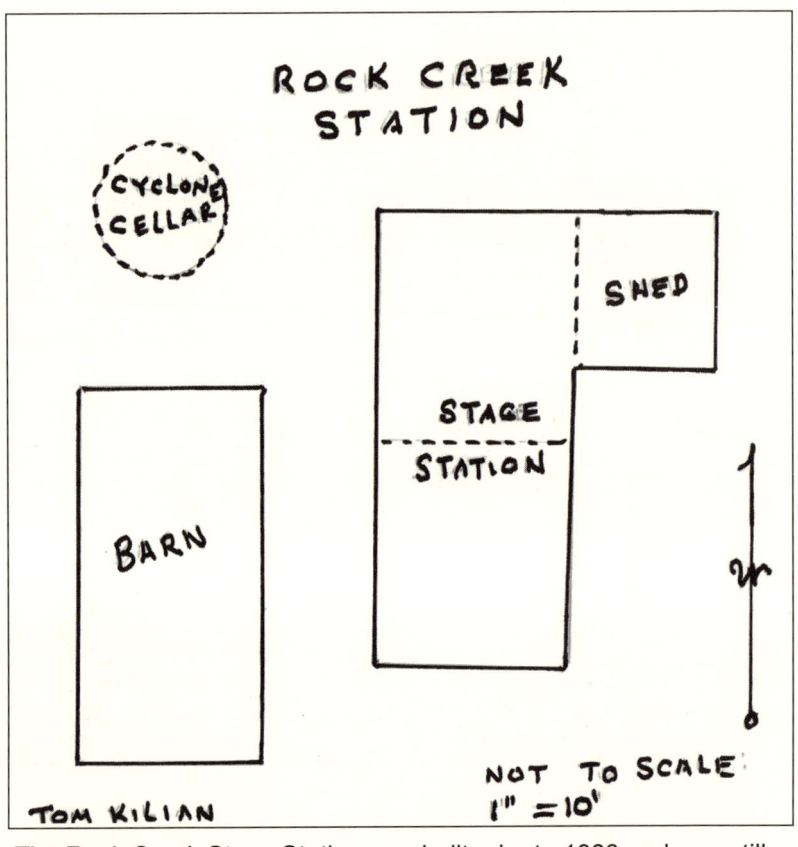

BARN

NOT TO SCALE
1" = 10'

TOM KILIAN

The Rock Creek Stage Station was built prior to 1883 and was still standing in 1903. Ward V. Kilian and his brother, Milo, played in the station as children. It was built of dimension lumber, with square nails and glass windows. There were two main rooms with a loft above, under a shed roof. The foundation was of native field stones. The building was in the shape of an "L," with a small shed attached. The barn was a simple, rough frame shell of a building. There was a cyclone cellar slightly south and west of the station. The roofs were shingled. The barn was about 200 feet south of the station building. The water source is uncertain and may have been Rock Creek, a short distance to the west. The station was located about 400 feet south of the trail.

These photos, taken at Wessington Springs, show stagecoaches that were typical of those traveling the trails in early Miner County.

A wrecked stage was the result of a run-away.

sent down the Mississippi to St. Louis and then back up the Missouri to the site of Crow Creek. Some of the Crow Creek Indians had been taken down to create a Santee Reservation in Nebraska when it was clear they could not make a living farming at Crow Creek. Some of those Indians, in turn, had walked overland to the present site of Flandreau and they were the beginning of that community. The site of some of their bark houses can still be seen in the Flandreau area. Dad said they found some arrowheads and other worked stones around their home on Rock Creek.

Old ruts from wagon wheels ran down through the grass to and across Rock Creek, were overgrown with grass but still visible. The stage station must have been used by the mail carriers who drove east and west from the Flandreau and Pipestone area out to Fort Thompson on the Missouri.

The Rock Creek Stage Station was built prior to 1883 and was still standing in 1903. It was built of dimension lumber, with square nails and glass windows. There were two main rooms with a loft above, under a shed roof. The foundation was of native field stones. The building was in the shape of an "L," with a small shed attached. The barn was simple, rough frame shell of a building. There was a cyclone cellar slightly south and west of the station. The roofs were shingled. The barn was about 200 feet south of the station building. The water source is uncertain and may have been Rock Creek, a short distance to the west. The station was located about 400 feet south of the trail.

Before the arrival of the railroads, there were other stage stations in the area. There was one on the old Theodore Esser place, south of Howard. It served for a time as a hotel and roadhouse and later converted into a farm house. Tradition says that stages came from the south to this point to connect with the stages running east and west. There were stage stations in the Forestburg area along the Jim River, and there likely was one or more between these and the one at Rock

Creek. Other stations are known to have existed around the lakes in the Madison area.

Before the Milwaukee Railroad was built, there was a stage line with federal contract to carry mail west from Flandreau, through Rock Creek and on to the James River near Forestburg and on to Wessington Springs.

In the fall of 1955, Dr. V. R. Nelson of Augustana College and I surveyed the area around the Rock Creek site. We went over the ground with a metal detector, one of the first ever used in South Dakota. Nelson and his staff had built the detector before such devices were available on the market. We found a small collection of old iron – wagon and harness hardware, mainly, which established the existence of activity in the area.

EARLY RADIO

In the 20's, following World War I, there were lots of changes in the society, in the nation and in Miner County, too. The first licensed broadcasts by radio stations began in 1920 and stations began to spring up all around the country. Among the early clear channel stations was WNAX in Yankton, established by the Gurney Seed Company in 1923 to promote their seeds and nursery stocks – and even some gasoline stations for a while.

My Grandfather decided radio was something he didn't want to miss and one day he came home to our house in Vilas and brought in a new radio. It was a grand thing, with a big walnut wooden case, full of tubes, some as large as small pop bottles. They had a filament in them that heated up and turned red when they were ready to operate. A separate cone-shaped paper speaker was placed in a heavy metal stand on top of the walnut cabinet.

Grandpa's radio was powered by a storage battery – one that would be a museum piece today. It was a large, heavy glass jar, open at the top and filled with a clear acid solution in which there were two metal plates or poles sticking down into the acid with wire running off them. Grandpa got a brace and bit and drilled two holes in the corner of the living room floor and ran wires into the basement below, where he stationed the battery. Grandmother Kilian was outraged that he would drill holes in the living room floor but her upset was all blown away with the wonder of what began to come forth on the radio: A WNAX Bohemian Band! The family was filled with awe and delight.

Grandpa was acquainted with D. B. Gurney, the founder of WNAX and the Gurney Seed and Nursery Company and not long after buying the radio, he went to Yankton and instructed us to be sure to listen to WNAX. Finally, he came on, greeted our family and said, "Hello, Tommy" and I was dazzled! Radio in those days wasn't regulated or programmed at all. At WNAX, there was a constant stream of people coming on the air to say hello to the home folks and "the friends and neighbors out in radioland!" Local amateur musicians would be put on to play and sing. A singing cowboy, George B. German, became a regional celebrity, singing songs like "Strawberry Roan" and "Little Old Sod Shanty on My Claim." Programming had yet to be organized and the commercial broadcasting world had yet to be born.

THE CRYSTAL SET

By the 30's, it was possible to buy radio kits for assembly at home. The least expensive were called "crystal sets" and they did not have a battery or any electric power. They consisted mainly of a little coil of copper wire and a condenser used for tuning, all connected to ear phones. There was no loud speaker. Crystal sets had to have a long antenna.

My brother and I bought a radio kit from a mail order company in Chicago. We cut out a little wooden board to mount the parts on. We strung a long copper wire over a distance of about half a block, between a large tree at the foot of our front yard and the second story of our house and ran a wire down from it to connect to the crystal set. A little tiny wire called a cat whisker was moved around on the surface of a rock crystal to produce a very clear radio signal in the earphones. It was like magic: we listened to large clear channel stations from all over the nation on that tiny radio, stations like KOA-Denver, WCCO-Minneapolis, WJR-Detroit and many more. We listened on the earphones when we were supposed to be sleeping and our parents never knew the difference!

This was the era of the golden age of the Big Band. The radio networks in the 1930's would pick up the music of these large dance bands from the hotel ballrooms all around the nation. They would switch every half hour to a different band, on into the night. We would listen to the bands of Tommy and Jimmy Dorsey, Harry James, Glen Miller, Cab Calloway, Artie Show, Claude Thornhill, Jimmy Lunceford, Sammy Kaye and the entire galaxy. We grew to know the styles and theme songs of dozens of bands and could recognize them upon hearing a few notes. It was a wonderful time.

We heard a lot of news and programming that many folks could not hear since radios were far from common in most homes in the 1920's and 1930's. Radio was the new means for connection with the outside world in the days before television and the internet were even imagined.

SLING-SHOT HEY-DAY

It is not clear whether the sling-shot enjoyed a special hey-day in Vilas or whether their use was simply more widespread. In any case, sling-shots were big among the kids in the Vilas area. They were a remarkable device and one that has since quietly vanished from the general scene.

Sling-shots were a product of a simple, less affluent time, in some part. To make a decent sling-shot, one had to have access to good tough, springy rubber. In the 20's and 30's that was easy. All auto tires had rubber tubes inside the tire – a kind of donut shaped balloon – which was a separate item that made it possible for the clumsy tires of that time to hold air. The rubber in them was wonderful. It was not hard to find old rubber tire tubes – every home had tubes that were blown out or so badly damaged, they could not be patched and re-used. These tubes supplied the critical feature of the sling-shot – the rubber bands that run from the crotch back to the leather sling pocket – the rock holder.

To make a good sling-shot, one began with a good wooden "Y" crotch from a tree that was tough, stringy wood that would stand pressure without breaking. A suitable wood might come from an ash, or willow or apple or even elm. Soft woods like cottonwood or boxelder would not do. The crotch was de-barked with a pocket knife and carefully trimmed to get down to the bare wood. Rubber bands were cut from the tubes, from about three to five-eights of an inch wide. It was important to cut the rubber band carefully so there were no nicks or cuts along the sides and so that the width was even for its whole length. Two notches, the width of the rubber band, were cut on each of the two prongs of the crotch and carefully trimmed down to be smooth. A leather patch was cut from an old leather glove or from the upper of an old shoe. Holes were cut in either side of it. The rubber bands were slipped through and securely tied with a strong string – shoemaker's linen or good grocer's string – that had been waxed with bee's wax or paraffin.

Choosing smooth stones of the right size and weight became an art for sling-shooting. Smooth rocks fly more reliably and straight or true. The weight of the stone had much to do with the distance it would go – heavier stones would carry better and farther. To pick good rocks, one would need to go to a gravel road to walk along picking up stones with a practiced eye. Smooth rocks of uniform size were easier to load into the leather sling and could be shot faster.

My brother was a master sling-shot maker. He not only made them according to the fundamentals described above, but he carved the crotches in many artistic ways and sand papered and soaked them in linseed oil until they became genuine works of arts. He produced sling-shots in great volume and gave them to the neighborhood kids, who never seemed to rise to his level of creative design, in their making. Sling-shots had a great advantage in their time – they were economical. They were made out of materials at hand at no outlay of cash. They worked wonderfully well to equip young boys with a hunting weapon, as a device for target practice and for general plinking. They could even serve as a protective device to discourage an aggressive dog or drive off small wild animals that became intrusive.

Learning to shoot a sling-shot came only with long continuous practice but it could come, with positive results. One could get good enough to hit a gopher or a sparrow, or a garter snake at some distance. Sling-shots were very useful in herding cows for one could keep a critter from wandering off by peppering her with stinging rocks. One could manage other animals the same way.

Sling-shots were handy. One could wrap the rubber bands around the prongs of the crotch and stick the crock in the back pocket of his overalls where the rubber bands would keep it from slipping out and getting lost and where it was always ready. Much has been lost in the summer life of kids who have never learned the joys of making and using good sling-shots.

THE RUBBER GUN WARS

During the 1930's, a major activity of the Vilas school boys were the Rubber Gun Wars. Rubber guns were not original with the Vilas kids but they took them to a high level of development – beyond any I am aware of in any other prairie village.

Rubber guns were made by the kids, from wood scraps cut out roughly to resemble real handguns. They varied greatly in size and design and were a reflection of the creative talents of the maker/owner. My brother, Austin, who was four years older than I, was an inspired builder of rubber guns. He made them not only for us but for other kids, on order. He was the community munitions dealer for kids.

Rubber guns had a device like a clothes pin on the back of the handle, which clamped and held a rubber band stretched from the front end of the "barrel" back to the clamp. The shooter simply pressed the clothespin/trigger and the heavy rubber band would fly off toward its target.

My brother built not only handguns, but long rifles and shotguns as well. These were of the general size and shape of these larger long barreled guns. Over some years time, the manufacture of rubber guns became quite sophisticated and hand guns were developed which could shoot four, five and even six "shots."

The rubber bands that were used with rubber guns were cut from old discarded automobile tire inner tubes. They were cut in varying widths depending on the size of the gun and the impact that the rubber band would produce when it hit the target. For really small handguns, like boot pistols or

Derringers a band was only a quarter inch wide. For the long guns – rifles – several rubber bands were tied together to make a band that could be stretched to the long length of the barrel. Brother Austin even built cannons. These were made with a small three-inch round fence post for a barrel, set on swivel mountings so that it could quickly be turned against a moving enemy. And, of course, the rubber bands were cut wider and heavier, as appropriate for cannon shells.

Having all of these armaments, the kids of the town would choose up sides as for a ball game and the two sides became the warring factions. Armed with rubber guns, they would fight in guerilla fashion all afternoon, running behind buildings, big rocks, down in ditches seeking to shoot the enemy. The side which succeeded in shooting the most enemies won the war for the day.

In the Rubber Gun Wars, the object was to shoot the enemy with a projected rubber band. If hit, the person was supposed to fall to the ground "dead." But because there were so few soldiers, it was not practical to have the shot persons remain dead and so they were given "live medicine." This imaginary drink was administered by a person fighting on the same side as the fallen comrade. Having been revived, he could then jump up and resume fighting!

These wars could range over the entire town in a given day. A favorite stronghold was in the barn at Hepner's, the home of three boys who were warriors from time to time. The barn had a large store of loose prairie hay in the loft. The kids obtained large cardboard boxes and wooden banana crates from the Hepner Store and built tunnels in the hay through which they could sneak up on an opponent. Great value was placed on the ability to sneak up on the enemy. Squads and patrols of gunfighters crept around behind trees, buildings, crawled along fence lines, moving with all the skills of Indian scouts. Stealth and surprise were important because of the short range of the rubber guns; it was necessary to get quite close to the enemy to insure a bodily hit.

The games resulted in the production of considerable creative ability among the kids since ingenuity paid off in devising new strategies and plans almost daily. One might secrete a squad on the roof of a garage or in the boughs of a large tree where traffic would likely pass.

The entire process was planned and directed by the kids themselves – no adults were involved in any way. The kids planned their own fun and built their own equipment. Such a system hardly seems possible today, where the practice is for adults to plan and closely oversee the use of the children's time, and the circumstances under which they play. An entire day of rubber gun wars where the parents had no clue as to where the kids were at a given time is today unthinkable. It is not clear that the kids are better served.

In fairness, the society has changed in so many ways. It is probably not possible to provide the unplanned freedom to kids that they were accorded then. The play of that day was a product of the time and place.

THE ERFMAN TRAGEDY

One of Vilas' and Miner County's most dramatic tragedies occurred in late July, 1930. Howard was holding its annual Harvest Festival, a typical prairie town celebration with a street carnival and novel attractions. Mr. and Mrs. Henry Erfman of Vilas and their five children were in Howard to attend the festival.

Among the attractions for the day were several barnstorming airplane pilots who were there to provide ten-minute rides and to fly air acrobatics to entertain attendees of the event.

Two of the Erfman children wanted to go for a ride and their tickets were purchased for them by an older brother. The plane, called "The Eagle Rock," was piloted by J. Merle Perigo, a licensed pilot from Huron, SD; the plane was owned by Rapid Airlines of Rapid City.

The plane took off in the face of an on-coming thunderstorm, the sky growing dark with heavy clouds. When the pane had attained an altitude of 600 feet, it suddenly encountered what the pilot later called a "miniature tornado." Strong turbulent winds turned the plane upside down. The two Erfman children, Clarence and Cecile, seated in an open cockpit and not strapped in, fell out of the plane to their deaths over farmlands north of the town. Cecile, a girl of 17 years, landed in a tree and her brother, Clarence, age 8, fell in a grain field. The bodies of both children were badly mangled.

The pilot landed the plane without difficulty or any damage. The tragedy was witnessed by several hundred on-lookers on the ground. An inquest was held and a panel of four citizens found that the event was an accident and not a fault of pilot error, as reported by the Miner County Pioneer, on August 1, 1930.

The tragedy was electrifying for the people of Vilas who knew the family and was especially shocking for the school children who were friends of the Erfman kids.

From the vantage point of the many years since that time, it seems curious that apparently no responsibility was assigned to the pilot or the airplane owners for not ensuring that the children were safely strapped in the open cockpit. What passed as an unhappy accident then would almost certainly result in liability litigation today. But it was a different society in 1930 in many ways, and these events emphasize the changes that have occurred.

READ, WRITE AND CIPHER

Since the 1930's, schools and their operation have changed more than most other systems in the community. At one time, there were about 80 rural schools in Miner County! They were mostly one-room schools for grades one through eight, taught by a single teacher. The teacher was usually a young woman who had received a state teaching certificate based on a few weeks of training in a "normal school" or college. There were three Normal Schools in eastern South Dakota during the first decades of the 1900's, at Madison, Aberdeen and Springfield. Tuition at Madison was $1.40 a month!

The rural school teacher had charge of everything that happened in the school. She was the classroom teacher for all eight grades in all subjects. She was the janitor and maintenance person, who came early in the winter to start the fire in the big iron stove to warm the classroom. She filled the coal bucket and the wood box. She carried water from the iron hand pump to fill the drinking "fountain," a ten–gallon stone jar with a tin dipper. She swept the floor and burned the waste paper. If the windows got washed, she washed them.

With varying success, some teachers were able to enlist students to help with the chores of running the place, that is: the kids would help carry water, wood or coal. They might help sweep the floors and shovel snow away from the doorway. They might wash off the blackboards. But it was the teacher who directed traffic and ran the entire show.

The teacher served as school nurse and counselor for the hurt and sick and sorrowing. She was the disciplinarian, to correct the unruly and keep order. She had to plan and conduct the special programs for Christmas and other holidays; to train the participants and to serve as hostess for the parents and other visitors to the school.

The teacher quite often was housed in a spare bedroom at the nearest farmstead and she took meals with the family there. It was not always the most restful and pleasant arrangement.

There was no indoor plumbing. There were two small wooden outhouses behind the school house. Sometimes there was a small barn in which horses driven or ridden by students could be kept during class hours.

Classes in given subjects were conducted with a row of chairs in the front of the room, to which students came from their desks for instruction to recite. Other students remained at their desks to study or, often, to listen to the class recitations.

So, in this system, a first grade student heard the goings-on for a class of fifth graders – and every other class taught at the school. While distracting, it was also instructive, since the kids heard much of what they were to learn in fifth grade long before they got there themselves! This arrangement has often been defended by persons who have held that the one-room school provided a very good education as a result of the repetitive process which students went through, by just being in the same room.

Among the classes for primary kids were those in penmanship, the process of learning to write by hand and to make the letters and numbers with a large round form. A process called the "Palmer Method" of teaching writing in this style was much in vogue and was the standard by which handwriting was judged. Language arts were regarded as very important then, and there were spelling and declamatory contests as a part of every school calendar.

Rural school rooms were quite uniform in their arrangement and equipment. There was a cast iron pot belly stove, usually in a corner of the room, placed on a heavy mat and a coal bucket or woodbox at hand. The student desks would be arranged in rows, with students seated one behind the other. The old desks had cast iron frames, seats of maple and hinged desktops. Underneath was space to store books, pencils, paper and other school supplies. In the upper right-hand corner of the desk top was an inkwell. It was a little metal capped glass cup of ink into which one dipped his steel pointed pen.

Often, the very old school desk tops had the initials of former students carved in the surface with pocket jackknives, some to the extent that the writing surface had become a rough and bumpy writing surface. A student who wanted to get a drink of water would have to raise his hand, be recognized by the teacher and given permission to leave his desk. Similarly, for trips to the outhouse, one had to raise his hand for the teacher's permission.

The teacher's desk was at the front of the room which allowed her to look over the rows of students and conduct the affairs of the day. Her desk would probably be in a corner of the front of the room, with a blackboard across the wall behind her. Above the blackboard hung large pictures of George Washington and Abraham Lincoln. To inspire the students to good citizenship, there was a national flag on a wooden flagstand. Somewhere in the room, probably in the back, was the "library," which consisted of a bookcase of open shelves. These contained a set of encyclopedias (if the school was fortunate) and copies of books of history, literature, geography. There might be books containing speeches of notable politicians, military persons and others held in public esteem. Near the bookshelves was a small stand or table with a copy of Webster's unabridged dictionary – a book about six inches thick. And nearby, would have been a globe, showing the oceans, continents, islands and other features of the earth's surface. That was about it for a classroom.

At the entry to the building, there was space along the walls for students to hang their coats, caps, scarves and mittens and to leave their overshoes or boots. Often, too, there would be shelves, where students could place their lunch buckets for safekeeping until the noon-hour. The kids ate

Above: The new Vilas school building housed elementary and high school classes.

Left: The Vilas church was southeast of the school.

Below: An early convertible at the Post Office.

outdoors in nice weather. The standard lunch bucket was a one-gallon metal pail, which had contained corn syrup or molasses before being recycled. Only well-to-do kids had lunch buckets made for that purpose with a thermos bottle for drinks. Lunch for most kids were large, heavy sandwiches of cold meat, peanut butter or sliced cheese. There would be an apple, orange or banana and piece of homemade cake or cookies. Kids were given an hour for lunch which meant they usually finished eating in time for some activity on the playground before "the bell rang." Sometimes, kids would trade items in their lunch pails for variety's sake. There was no "lunchroom" or space set aside for eating lunches. One ate wherever he was the most comfortable, inside or out, depending on the weather.

On the Vilas school grounds, there were swings with metal chains holding the seats to a heavy standard of metal posts. There were teeter-totters of heavy wooden planks set on a heavy metal frame, and there was a merry-go-round, powered by kids who would get inside the framework of metal and push, round and round, fast as they could go.

The playground equipment would get a frantic workout during recess times. Ballgames and other games like winter sports (fox and goose in the snow) would take longer to play and were generally done during the noon hours or after school in the afternoon.

Kids would also range around in the grasslands surrounding the school in the spring, looking for wild onions. One could chew the onions which would give one a most powerful breath and when a number of kids did this all at once, the entire classroom would hang heavy with this unpleasant onion smell. There were even excursions off of the school grounds onto adjoining grasslands, to hunt gophers and to catch them with a snare made of heavy cord.

A couple of my grubby little friends and I got into serious trouble with the superintendent and with our parents when we took some of our dead gophers and put them in the heat ducts that carried the hot air from the basement furnace to all of the classrooms. The entire school reeked to high heaven with the terrible smell of these little dead critters; school was dismissed that day to allow the authorities to get to the bottom of the matter. They got to the bottom and eventually to us and we suffered for it, as we should have.

Discipline was often quick and by present-day standards – very severe. On one occasion, I remember, being called to the front of our classroom along with several cronies and the teacher made us hold out our hands, palms up, while she beat on them with a heavy, blue 18 inch ruler with a steel edge! Our hands didn't bleed, but they were so swollen and stiff that it was hard to close our fingers. Another time, the same teacher laid on us with a coil of rubber hose, (the sort used in chemistry classes) and whipped us! We deserved it. And, there was no outrage from parents or talk of lawsuits or legal actions against the school. The common expectation in those years was: "if you get a lickin' in school, you'll get another one when you get home!" So kids assumed that they were being justly punished for their crimes and that "they had it comin'."

Parent visits to the school were very rare and usually confined to attendance at Christmas programs or special events. Communication between parents and students was in the form of "report cards" filled out by the teacher or, rarely, in notes exchanged and carried by the students.

Other school visitors during the year were the County Nurse and the County Superintendent. These were real occasions and the teacher and the pupils tried to present themselves as best they could, so their school would be well regarded.

In the early 30's, the end of the Vilas school year in the spring was celebrated by a school picnic for everyone, which was held in an ash grove along the east bank of Rock Creek, a short distance north of the intersection of it with Highway #34. It was an occasion to which the kids looked forward to with great anticipation, not only because it was the end of school, with a summer of freedom ahead, but because of the picnic food and drinks.

The ash grove was an attractive place – lots of shade trees and prairie birds such as the American and Arkansas Kingbirds, red-headed woodpeckers, doves and many others. The grass under the trees was clipped short by grazing cows pastured there, and made a wonderful spot for playing games.

Beside the normal picnic fare of hot dogs, potato salad, beans and ice cream was served out of large metal cans enclosed in heavy cloth cases, to keep them cold. For drinks there was a variety of fruit flavored soda pops: orange, cherry, strawberry, lemon and grape and a new drink, not yet common called Coca Cola.

At one Vilas school picnic, watermelons were served and one of the older boys secretly cut a plug out of one of the melons, poured in a healthy dose of grain alcohol and put the plug back in when it had soaked in or had been absorbed. News of this audacity spread among the kids like wildfire and all those who had watermelon either felt or feigned the effects and imagined themselves as being drunk on melon!

The ash grove along the creek is gone now with barely an old snag or two left to mark the location but in its time, it was a wonderful place.

Even though the equipment and room arrangements were the same as most one-room schools, the school at Vilas was considered to be a "town" school and thus more sophisticated and advanced.

Vilas had a new school building which was dedicated in 1928 with three large classrooms, one each for lower and upper grades and one for the high school. Vilas had a two-year high school, one of very few in the state. It operated for a number of years but closed in 1936, which was the year I was supposed to enroll in high school. Vilas High School students had to go to Howard and so I attended all four years of high school there.

There were no school buses in those years. If one went to a school, it was his business to get there, however. For me, that often meant riding the Milwaukee passenger train going east for the three and one-half miles between Vilas and Howard. I would walk from home to the railroad depot and get on the train, and walk to the school in Howard.

I could return to Vilas in the late afternoon on a west bound train. Getting to after-hours events was more complicated for we would have to drive the family Ford or Studebaker, ride with other kids or hitchhike.

The faculty – the teachers – at Howard were really very good, in retrospect. Perhaps most memorable was an English teacher whose name was Genevieve West. She was outstanding and we received great background in English and literature – and a respect for learning in general. I had a good Latin teacher, Golda Gaskins. While I was terrified by her, I learned a great deal in her classes.

The entire high school student body was seated in a large study hall – our "home room," for we had no other. Again, there were long rows of desks with the freshmen along the east walls, and progressing until, as a senior, one got a desk along the west wall, where there were windows nearby. There was a platform or stage in the front of the room on which was a desk for the teacher who was the overseer of the moment. There, also, would come the superintendent of the school, in a dark suit and with a pompous manner, who would lecture us on how to behave or whatever he felt would benefit us to know. We were fairly orderly and well behaved as I remember, though we were very adept at passing notes back and forth between our friends. These hand-written notes were the "text-messages" of our day and were probably no more important.

There was no food served at the school – we carried our lunches as we had all through grammar school. The Howard kids who lived in town could go home for noon meals but all others had to bring their lunches. Lunches were eaten in cars parked along the edge of the school ground – or, in very nice weather, on the lawn.

Howard High School had a number of special rooms for teaching. There was a room for biology (to carve up frogs and such). There was a room with equipment for chemistry and physics. There were no audio-visual aids such as films or slides or recordings used in classes. All of the instruction was given by the teacher or from the textbook. There was a band room to practice instrumental and band. Speech and drama events were practiced on the stage of the study hall. And, there was a small gym for basketball with seats for spectators, set back into the south and east walls, above the playing floor for basketball. There was no football played in those days, because a student was supposed to have died during a game or practice in earlier years.

The high school gym was the scene of a great many social events, parties and especially dances. The annual prom was staged there, when the place was transformed into a fairyland of crepe paper and balloons. Music was played on a phonograph and it all seemed wonderful.

My high school years were generally happy years. There were about 30 kids in my class and we got along well together. There were the regular school activities and events, but we had lots of picnics and dances and hang-outs of our own which were really fun. One or another of the kids was usually able to come up with a car which we could use to get to a picnic ground or to a lake shore or dance hall.

Following commencement, which was held in the Legion Hall, our class scattered out over the world and we had no idea how dramatically our lives and the whole world society would change. That period was the beginning of the end for the rural society we had known. Technology was changing everything and it would never be the same.

THE METHODIST CHURCH

The only church in Vilas was Methodist Episcopal, a tiny white frame building in the northwest corner of town. It was a kind of community church open to anyone who would come. Folks with strong denominational persuasions generally had to go to Howard or elsewhere. The road past the front of the church ran to the school house, the last building in the northwest part of town.

The church was of simple design, with a roofed entrance on the southwest corner, and a modest louvered square steeple directly above. Inside, the congregation sat in pews facing an altar on the north wall. Other than hymn books, a piano and lectern, there were no other furnishings.

Sunday school was held by grouping the various grades in sections of the pews apart from each other, since the tiny building did not afford separate rooms.

The church was served by preachers who came from Howard. In the period between the two World Wars, the Reverends E. F. Kurtz and E. E. Whiteside led the services.

The Vilas Ladies Aid of the M. E. Church were the most active members of the congregation, who periodically held chicken suppers and bazaars in the Odd Fellows Hall, since it had a kitchen and a large serving area. As in most rural churches, the men were silent spectators, who attended church but who rarely sang or actively responded to the services. They tended to be more stolid, silent and reserved and to feel the church was women's work.

In general, the services were happy occasions – the pastors preached love and warmth; worshipers sang the old, camp meeting hymns, like "Church in the Wildwood," "Blessed Assurance" and "Blest be the Tie." It was a warm, forgiving place, made up of earnest, honest people.

FARMING

THE FAMILY FARM

Before the second World War, in the 1930's and earlier, the area in Miner County around Vilas was an area of small farms. Surveyors laid out Miner County as a square with 20 square townships, each with 36 mile-square sections. The sections were divided into quarter sections of 160 acres each. Thus, a "quarter" was the standard popular unit of farm land and, in those times, almost every quarter section in the county had a farmstead with a family living there.

It must be understood that large production agriculture had not yet been invented. These small 160 acre farms were basically subsistence operations farms. Their purpose was to provide a home, food and shelter for the family – to provide a place to raise the food the family needed, to provide a home as shelter against the weather. Farms were not seen as a business in the current sense, as an investment expected to make a profit and return on investment.

Virtually all farms were diverse stock and grain farms. They would regularly plant crops of small grains, as wheat, barley, rye and oats, and corn and possibly fodder. The crops were rotated with corn or grains planted in alternate years. Nearly all farms had a pasture area of native grasses to graze cattle and horses and some land devoted to producing wild hay and/or alfalfa.

The farms were quite uniform in the buildings included on the farmstead. The house was a wood frame, usually two story, square or rectangular with a wood shingled roof with an attendant outhouse. There would be a barn with a second story hayloft, and stalls and stanchions for horses and

Pulling plows through the tough prairie virgin sod required the power of the huge steam tractors. A water wagon is standing by.

The man on the platform operates the levers to raise and lower the plows.

cattle. There was a hog house with small outdoor pens and a chicken house, with roosts and nests for chickens that were given free-range of the farmyard. There was a granary with bins for small grains and a corn crib to store ear corn. There might be an additional large open shed in which to park and repair farm machinery used in the fields. There could be additional small sheds to house sheep or turkeys or geese or other farm animals. Generally, the house was painted white and the farm buildings red. There was a windmill, with a stock tank for water for man and beast. All of the machinery for farming was horse drawn. An average complement of farm machines included: a wagon with a grain box; a hayrack; a buggy, one or more plows; a disc, a drag, a corn planter, for checkrow planting; a one and a two-row corn cultivator, a grain seeder and binder and a corn binder. Smaller items around the farm yard included two-wheel carts, stone boats and wheel barrows.

Most farms had a tool shed, to house the collection of hand tools needed to keep the farm in operation. This included a mixture of carpenter, blacksmith and maintenance equipment, necessary to fix wooden and metal items of great variety. Most farmers were noted for their ingenuity in fixing broken things and for inventing and designing new tools for specified tasks. There also would be fence building and mending equipment and a great range of small specialized handtools related to raising certain animals, for crops and gardening.

Farmsteads where the resident was the land owner usually had a substantial grove of trees for a windbreak and for ornamental purposes. The grove served as a source of kindling for the kitchen cookstove, as a source of handles for harmers, hatchets and other tools. Not least, the farm grove might serve as a tiny hunting preserve to provide a fat cottontail or a game bird for the kitchen pot.

There were no hybrid or engineered varieties of plants. The seed for all crops was collected from the best of the prior year's crop or from a neighbor's. There were no commercial fertilizers in general use and purchased fertilizer was simply not a part of the farming plan, or it was an expense. Fertilizer came from manure, hauled to the fields in spreaders. And, since the machines were horse drawn, there was no expense for gasoline for tractors, combines or other engines. The substitute energy was human and horse muscle.

This accumulation of the buildings and equipment evolved over a couple generations. The pioneer ancestors would have begun farming with a bare skeleton of this inventory, beginning possibly with a sod shanty or claimshack, a rough animal shelter, a walking plow, some shovels and hand scythes for harvesting.

Not every farm had all of these items. There was liberal borrowing and lending back and forth and even joint ownership of some larger items, such as a threshing machine.

With many variations, there was an exchange of labor for some projects where extra hands would help, in harvesting, framing up a new shed or digging a cistern or cyclone cellar.

Frugal management and long hours of hard work usually paid off, and barring some serious illness or other misfortune, the family might succeed in gaining some cash through the year's efforts. Any gains in cash would almost certainly be devoted to improving the farm – paying off debts or mortgages with the goal of debt-free ownership, or building buildings, buying machines or even adding acres of adjoining farmland. The central goals were to feed and house the family, educate the children and build ownership and equity.

The reality of farm life, for people in the drought years of the 1930's, was a bare subsistence at best: enough feed to keep the animals alive and bare necessity food and clothes for the family. For many, the demands were too great. Unable to raise enough money to make ends meet, they packed up the things they could carry or strap onto the old family car and they left – for California or Oregon. Once as a young boy, out hunting gophers with my friend, we walked into a farmyard to get a drink at the windmill. The family was packing up to leave and we watched as they finished, got into their old car and drove off, leaving the doors swinging in the wind! They were headed for Oregon, where the valleys were said to be bulging with ripe fruit, the grain fields and the pastures lush. They waved goodbye as they drove off, leaving two puzzled little boys watching them disappear down the dirt road toward their new world.

THE HAY MAKERS

Harvesting began in the summer with the cutting and storing of hay – the grasses and native plants that would be cut for food for the livestock through the winter ahead.

Hay making was done on tracts of land with native grasses that had not been plowed up. These often included land that was lower, along creeks and wetlands where there was more moisture. It was often land with rises or hills or with low spots which made it less desirable for crop land. And, if grasslands were full of rocks, left by glaciers thousands of years ago, and hilly as well, they were left for pasture for cattle, horses and sheep since they could not be mowed because of the stones.

The wild hay grass was cut with a horse-drawn mower, an iron, two-wheeled machine on which the driver sat low to the ground and from which projected off to the right side, an iron frame to enclose a sickle bar, with sharp, triangular cutting knives. A system of gears running off the wheels of the mower pulled the sickle back and forth rapidly as it moved over the surface of the ground and cut the hay which would lay on the grass behind the mower. The mower was pulled by two horses.

It was quite common for the mower to scare up meadowlarks, killdeers and other small birds that built their nests in the grasses. Often, these nests were destroyed by the sickle or if they survived they would probably be abandoned by the bird family as a result of the disturbance. Occasionally, the nests of a pheasant or grouse would be broken up in the same way. The birds, especially larks and killdeer, would usually perform their fluttering, crippled ruse, flying a short spurt ahead and landing, to try to lure the intruder away, but this ruse was well known.

Following the mower, would come the hay rake, most often a "dump rake," which had an array of iron tines or teeth curved in a half circle with the bottom riding lightly over the ground. The cut hay/grasses were caught in the teeth of the rake and carried along until the operator touched a tripping device with his foot and the rake teeth would raise up and leave a pile of hay behind, with the rake dropping down to gather up another batch.

Following the rake, came a "bucker," a wooden frame with a flat bed of long pointed shafts of hardwood arranged to pick up the piles of hay left by the rake and carry them along to a point where it was intended to build a hay stack. An alternate way of picking up the dumps of hay left by the rake was with a hay rack. A large box-like frame of wooden slats riding on a four-wheeled running gear of a farm wagon pulled by two horses would be driven around the hay field. Men with pitch forks would pitch the hay into the rack and haul to the site of the haystack. Or, they might haul it to a barn at the farmyard for storage.

In the field, a haystack was built by men pitching the hay up to the top of a growing pile where a man would arrange it to form a stack. Or, the hay was raised by a "stacker," a

The driver of the hay mower has a dump rake behind him to pile up the newly mown hay. Note the fly nets on the horses.

Horses supplied the power to lift the piles of hay delivered to the growing stack by the hay bucker, at the left of the photo.

wooden machine with a scoop made up of wooden tines or shafts that would scoop up the pile of hay delivered to it by the bucker. Then a long wooden arm would raise the load of hay to the top of the stack. A well-built hay stack was arranged and sloped to shed rain, allowing the grass to cure in the dry prairie air.

No one who has ever been present at haying time can ever forget the smell of new-mown prairie hay. It is a combination of a half dozen or more native grasses and aromatic plants that grow on the prairie like white sage, curly dock and gumweed. It is the kind of smell that sinks deep in one's psych and which will always mean "prairie."

Once put up, hay stacks became the watchtower and resting place for various prairie hawks who would perch on them and watch for mice, that made their home in the grass, as well as the striped gopher, garter and bull snakes and other smaller critters.

Those who ran the mower and rakes in a hayfield had a special opportunity to become acquainted with the plants and animals of the grasslands. They had to be alert for the large holes dug by the badgers, skunks and fox. They learned how and where all of these creatures lived and became acquainted with their habits and ways of life.

THE THRESHERS

Among the changes that technology has brought about on the prairie farm is the process of harvest. Today, we wait for the crop to mature, to turn brown and dry, and then in an afternoon, two or three huge machines can cut the crop, separate the grain from the chaff and straw, deposit the grain into large waiting trucks and all be gone by sundown.

In the 1920's, the whole process was different. Then, when the crop was dry and ready to cut, a grain binder was pulled onto the field by three or four horses. It had a large wooden reel made of wooden slats which would push down the standing stalks of grain and push them into a sickle bar that cut them. The action of the reel pushed the cut stalks over and laid them flat on a wide moving canvas platform which revolved round and round on wooden rollers. The grain stalks were fed into a catcher, which, when packed full enough, automatically wrapped a hemp twine binder around the bundle of grain and cast it out onto a catcher. When the catcher contained a load of six or more bundles, it dropped them on the ground as the binder moved on.

The operator of a grain binder had to be alert – many things could go wrong: the canvas/roller systems might get stuck or tear loose; the grain might plug up in the area forming the bundles; the device which tied the bundles wouldn't work right and the loose grain would be cast out onto the ground; any of a number of metal chains that drove the cogwheels that transferred power to the different functions of the machine would break or jump the track. So, the operator had to be a combination of repair man and saint.

Following the binder through the fields were one or more young men, called "shockers," who moved from one pile of bundles to the next, setting them up with the grain heads uppermost, into small, conical stacks with the bundles inclined toward the center and leaning against each other for support. Building shocks that would stand in a strong wind was important, to keep the grain up off the ground in case of rain. Experienced and speedy shockers were much in demand and hired out to follow the binders around the community.

When the shocking was done, the entire field was dotted with shocks and would look much like a field today covered with large round bales of hay. The shocks stood in place until it was time for threshing.

Threshing was a time of hustle and bustle. Threshing was done by a group of farmers who banded together and who

A field of barley in the shock is drying, waiting for the bundle racks which will haul them to the threshing machine.

A grain binder cuts grain and ties it into bundles for the shockers who follow.

moved with the tractor and threshing machine from farm to farm. These farmers formed what was called a "threshing ring."

Threshing the small grain crops underwent a remarkable evolution during the generation prior to the 1920's. The first threshing machines were powered by horses hitched to a long heavy bar, which stuck out from a gear box. The horses pulled the bar round and round in a circle. The power was transferred to the threshing machine through a system of shafts and gears to turn the machinery. This system was replaced by huge steam tractors which powered the machine with pulleys and belts. The owner of the steam engine and thresher would go from farm to farm and thresh grain in stacks that had been built from bundles. The threshing machine would be pulled up along side the stacks and the grain bundles pitched into the thresher by men with pitchforks on top of the stacks.

In earlier times, before 1920, the first tractors to power threshing machines were these huge steam-driven engines, a few relics of which remain today to cause wonder and awe at threshing bees and harvest festivals around the region. One such steam engine was owned by a man named Oscar Krause, who lived northwest of Vilas. The story was told that one day he was pulling his thresher along a dirt township road north of Vilas when he came to a railroad grade which rose up sharply to the railroad track and fell off sharply on the other side. Krause drove his big steam engine up and over the track and just started down with the threshing machine still moving up behind him. Something about the sharp angle of the road grade or the way in which the thresher was hooked on to the engine resulted in a hang-up: the engine pointing down on one side and the thresher coming up on the other. The threshing machine was stuck and refused to budge.

The threshing rig of Oscar Krause includes a steam tractor, a threshing machine and a water wagon.

A man pitching bundles of grain into the threshing machine provides the flow of grain into the wagon, at the left.

A growing pile of straw results from the work of the threshers and grain haulers.

Loads of grain wait in line for deposit of the new crop at the elevators.

Then, in true melodramatic sequence, Oscar heard a distant whistle: a train was coming! Oscar said, "I had no choice...I gave her the juice...and, I broke the (hitch) pin..." and the engine rolled forward and the thresher rolled backward, back down the slope and cleared the track, just as the train came roaring through the middle! The iron pin which Oscar's powerful steam engine broke was at least an inch thick and the story helped to create a local legend.

Power to run the threshing machines came from long belts running on flywheels and pulleys from the tractors to the machine. The thresher had feeders full of chopping knives, into which the grain bundles were thrown. The machine knocked the grain loose from the stalks, ran the grain over the screens which sifted out the chaffs and weed seeds and other foreign matter. It fed the clean grain into waiting wagons and blew the grain stalks – the straw – out through the long metal pipe called the "blower" and piled it up into a straw stack.

By the 1920's, the huge steam tractors had been largely replaced by smaller threshing machines powered by gasoline driven tractors, which could be moved more quickly and gave power to smaller threshing machines with a feeder about 22 to 26 inches wide, as opposed to the steam-driven ones with feeders of 36 to 40 inches wide.

A "threshing ring," was composed of from six to nine neighboring farmers, who owned the machinery and who worked only to complete their own threshing. It was a much speedier process and could be completed in from two to three weeks. Formerly, with the big steam rigs, working on grain stacks already in place, the threshing season could last from eight to ten weeks.

The newer, smaller threshing machines and gasoline tractors were well suited to the system of leaving shocked grain in the field to dry until ready to thresh. When the threshing machine and tractor arrived on the farm, a crop of fast-moving bundle racks would swarm into the grain field.

The grain bundles were hauled off of the field in wood frame hayracks or "bundle" racks on a regular farm wagon running gear and pulled by two horses. Operators of bundle racks drove their horses from one set of shocks to the next, tossing the bundles into their rack with a pitchfork until the rack would hold no more. Then they would jump up on the rack and trot their horses to the thresher.

They fell in line behind bundle racks already lined up, waiting to pull forward and pitch their bundles into the feeder with the chopping knives on the threshing machine. One or two men were stationed at this point to help pitch bundles from the racks into the thresher and to clean up bundles that may have fallen to the ground in the haste of unloading. These were called "spike pitchers" and they sometimes rode along on the rack back to the grain field to help load bundles onto the rack and bring them in to the machine. So, the bundle racks would go, back and forth, until the field was all clear of grain shocks.

In those days, every farm raised several types of small grains, usually wheat, barley and oats – and sometimes, rye and even spelt. When the grain was threshed out, it was fed into a wagon with high side boards which, when full, was pulled by two horses to the farmer's granary, a building with a number of bins to which the grain could be shoveled with large scoop shovels by the wagon driver and assistants at the granary into one or another of these bins, where it would stay, waiting for use for animals feed or rarely to be ground into flour to make bread for the farm family.

The small grains hauled away from the thresher to the farmer's granary were critical in providing feed for his animals during the late fall, winter and early spring. Oats for the horses, barley for the pigs were important. Grains not required for feed were hauled to town and sold at the elevator.

Straw piles were valuable assets in the days of farming with horses. Straw was used as bedding for horses, cows and all the farm animals. It helped keep animals warm in winter. The straw was sometimes used to make nests for chickens to lay eggs and as mulch for garden plants. It was used to bank up the foundations of buildings to keep out the cold. When tractors replaced horses and combines replaced threshing machines, the straw pile disappeared into history.

All the tasks in threshing were performed as fast as possible and this provided opportunity for the more macho of the young farm hands to demonstrate muscle: who could load and unload the fastest; who could get out to the field, load up and come back the quickest, driving the most spirited horses. And, who could do these things with flair and careless energy, so as to stand out in the group.

Even a small threshing ring included at least eight or ten or more men. As they moved from farm to farm, with their big machines and entourage of bundle racks, grain wagons and assorted other vehicles, they needed to be fed. So, as there were crews of men, so were there crews of women – wives and daughters – who traveled from farm to farm to help the hostess/wife to prepare for noon and afternoon lunches to be brought out to the site of the threshing machine. They would also bring jugs of drinking water, perhaps lemonade and certainly coffee to the entire threshing crew. But their real and major task was the preparation of a huge noon meal for all. This might include fried chicken, complete with gizzards and livers, or home-canned meat and bowls of gravy and mashed potatoes, green peas or beans, huge platters of homemade bread or rolls, plates of butter, jam or jelly, pickles and probably pie – fruit, raisin or mince. Men who expended prodigious energy could eat prodigious amounts of food and it took a community to do it all successfully.

Women developed reputations as great cooks or managers and go-getters by their performance in such settings.

Provision had to be made for the hot, dusty threshers to "wash-up" before the meal and this meant setting up benches with basins, soap and towels so they could slosh off their arms and faces, covered with the fine dust from the grain fields and from the threshing machine. All in all, small grain threshing was like a minor tempest when it hit the farm.

The contrast of all this with the systems now used to harvest small grains and beans are dramatic. The farmer owner may do little but issue instructions to contracted combine crews and truckers. The housewife may work in town and never meet the "threshers." Technology has changed life in enormous ways.

THE CORN HUSKERS

The last large harvesting job on the 1920-30 farm was corn. Every quarter section farm had a corn field, to provide corn to feed the pigs and chickens, next year's seed and maybe some to sell. Corn harvest began when green corn stalks were cut for silage. Corn was cut with a "corn binder," which did the same job as a small grain binder except it had to cut the much heavier stalks of corn and tie them into bundles. The bundles were dropped off in the field behind the binder in the same way as grain bundles, except they were much larger and heavier. Shockers came along on foot and set up the corn shocks in the same fashion. Standing the bundles on the cut ends they propped them up against each other to form a conical shock. Setting up the bundles of corn stalks in shocks kept the stalks up off the ground and allowed them to dry out. Finally, the corn bundles would be gathered up and hauled to the farm yard, to be stacked up in a stockpile for winter animal feed.

Some families used to plant pumpkins and squash in between corn rows and in the fall, the orange dot of pumpkins could be seen among the shocks.

Corn that was not cut for silage was left to stand until it was thoroughly dry, in order to pick the ears of corn from the stalks. Dry ones broke free more easily.

There were corn picking machines that could be pulled through the field by horses to pick the ears off the corn stalks and feed them into a wagon. However, most small farmers, especially in the earlier times, picked corn by hand. To do this, they waited long as they dared, after the first frosts and before the first snowfalls.

Corn was picked by a farmer walking along beside a wagon which had a high "bang-board" on the side of the wagon farthest from him. This board was used to stop the ears thrown up into the wagon and allow them to drop down into the wagon box. A small leather glove-like "husking hook" was worn on the picker's hand to help break the corn ears from the stalk. A skilled corn husker could walk along beside the moving wagon which the horses pulled slowly forward and keep a steady barrage of corn ears flying up, hitting the bang board and dropping into the wagon box.

Cornhuskers developed great skill and competitions arose between the fastest ones. Today, there are vestigial corn husking contests still held to demonstrate how it was done and to provide entertainment and diversion in rural communities.

Sometimes, early snow falls required picking corn in the snow, which could mean a cold, exhausting day, with red noses and cheeks and chapped, cracked hands for the corn pickers.

Some wagons were driven into an open alley way in an airy, slatted walled building called a "corn crib" which would keep the corn dry with air passing through the slatted walls of the corn bins and with a dry roof overhead. Wagon loads

Corn picking by hand. Corn ears were thrown at the high bang board and dropped in the wagon pulled by mules.

Early mechanical corn pickers were heavy and required a lot of horse power.

A mechanical corn sheller driven by a stationary engine. A corn crib is in the center; a cob pile at the left.

Horses pulling a corn cultivator have nose bags and blankets to protect them from savage flies.

of corn were hauled into the farm yard and the corn ears shoveled into outdoor bins made of wooden slats or heavy metal wire, to be stored for use later.

During the winter or early spring, old-time farmers would go to the corn cribs and select the largest, well-formed ears to be used for seed in the spring. They would shell the kernels from the cobs with a hand-cranked corn sheller and sack up the kernels in gunny sacks. In the spring, the sacks would be hauled to the field with the corn planter.

The corn cobs when free of their kernels were saved in piles or bins for use as fuels in the kitchen cook stoves on the farm. Cobs were a clean and reliable heat source for winter cooking and home heating. Cobs were carried into the home in large wire baskets or in wooden "bushel" baskets and set near the big cast iron kitchen cook stove.

There were other uses for cobs. If the farm had a surplus of them, they were sometimes used to fill in mud holes around the farmyard to form a more solid footing. Corncobs were even used by farm women to make "corn cob jelly," a flavorful light amber or rose colored jelly which used the sugars contained in the cob to make a very tasty spread for jelly sandwiches or toast. Corn cob jelly may still be found in displays of rural crafts at fairs.

Cobs supplied a variety of needs, such as stoppers in jugs, handles for tools, and a variety of uses which required an item of that size.

THE PLAGUES OF THE 1930'S

Some of the most memorable years in Miner County history came in the 1930's, with the Great Drought and Depression. The drought began in earnest in 1931. Most of the 1920's had been years of adequate rainfall, with several years of record crop yields. The last good corn year was in 1928.

The last years of the 1920's were getting more dry, evidently getting ready for the 1930's. The years 1931 and '32 were very dry with little or no crops. The historic dust storms began in 1933 and the most dramatic of all came on November 13, 1933, sometimes called the "Armistice Day Storm." Great clouds of dust rolled in from the northwest and the sky was dark as night: lights from autos could not penetrate it, for it was a physical cloud. People were awed by a new weather world they had never seen before.

The dust was as fine as flour and it crept into houses everywhere. For the next two years until the middle of 1935 there were many storms, with a number nearly as bad as the November storm of 1933. Dust covered the window sills, blowing in around the dried-out wooden window frames. It permeated the whole house and settled on the dining tables: so that women would turn the plates and dishes upside down to keep the dust off of them until a meal was served. And, when dishes were raised from the table, they would leave a lighter imprint of the table cloth below. People awakened from a night's sleep to find a white outline of their heads on the pillow! Wiping and washing away dust became an unending task.

The great dust storms were not confined to Miner County or even the state; the winds blew dust across the states to the east and even reached Washington, D. C. They ranged from North Dakota to Texas.

The dry soil and incessant wind had an abrasive and cutting effect on the surface of the farm fields and created even more dust so that the soil drifted and shifted. One of the few wild plants that could tolerate the extreme drought was the Russian thistle. They would grow into large round balls, die and dry out, break loose from their roots and roll with the wind.

The thistles would roll until they came to a barbed wire fence and catch in the wires. The dust would be slowed and

A black Blizzard in 1934.

Cattle pens drifted full of dust.

A farm fence buried in drifted dust.

would build up along the fence of thistles much like a snow fence creates its own drifts. Some fences caught so much dirt that they drifted over and disappeared beneath it. There were instances where cattle escaped their pasture by walking up over the dirt drifted fence, much as they could with winter hard, frozen snow banks that sometimes covered the fences.

In general, the winds blew daily from the southwest – day after day. They would go down at night and start up again with the new day. "Southwest Wind" became a by-word among the farmers who were facing ruin because of it.

Water for livestock became a serious problem for some since the water in ponds and wetlands was long since dried and gone and the only water was from the windmills. Water from the deep wells continued to be plentiful, since irrigation and pivots had not yet been devised to lower the water tables. Water at the windmill was cool, clear and reliable.

Government relief programs were first begun for farmers in 1932 and increased steadily through 1936. The federal government created the Works Progress Administration, called the "WPA" by everyone, to provide work and a tiny income to destitute farmers. Around Vilas and in Miner County, most of the work consisted of putting gravel on dirt roads of the countryside. Farmers had to provide a wagon, with a platform made of loose 2 x 6 inch planks and with low siding boards. This was used to haul gravel directly from sandpits that were opened along creek beds and drainage areas. The farmers met at a timekeep's shack at the sandpit in the morning to check in, would then drive into the sand pit and shovel their wagon full of sand and then plod off to the site along a road and dump out the gravel by tipping the loose boards of the wagon's sand box.

There were many other outdoor improvement projects undertaken by the WPA, including the building of small bridges and culverts along roads, placing rip-raps of stone

During the 1930's drouth, miniature dust dunes were formed around plants anchored by their roots. Winds filled with abrasive dust cut the soil to form more dust.

Dust caught in Russian thistles in a fence line created a mound which covered the fence.

along creek banks and lake shores to stop erosion, building parks and playgrounds and many other public projects.

Relief programs were provided to serve nearly all people in the area with food commodities such as cheese, butter, flour, cereals, and fruits in season. Some farmers received hay and grain for livestock.

Along with the drought came terrible heat in the summers; daily temperatures often over 100 degrees F, were common for days at a time. On the worst days, a blazing sun drove the thermometer up over 112 to 115 degrees. Soil in the farm fields was as dry as ashes – in 1934, seeds planted did not even sprout – they just lay in the dirt like gravel.

Tools and iron objects out in the sun were too hot to hold. One day my brother and I fried some eggs on the iron manhole cover of our cistern. They fried as quickly as if in a skillet on a stove.

In some ways the 1930's could be compared to the Biblical Plagues of Egypt: there were many unusual burdens to be borne by the people. Among the plagues were great clouds of grasshoppers that came in numbers that darkened the sky, casting a veil over the sun. They were huge yellow ones and they were ravenous. The summer of 1935 they were particularly bad; there were instances where they ate an entire field of corn in a single day, down to the stumps of the stalks. They ate the grass, the gardens – everything green.

The grasshoppers ate almost everything in their path. Housewives learned not to leave clothing out on their clothes lines for the hoppers would chew holes in them and leave only tattered rags. They ate the soft grey covering on the cedar fence posts. They even chewed into the hard hickory pitch fork handles leaving them pitted, rough and full of slivers. Such poor crops as might grow would never mature for if the burning sun and searing wind didn't get them, the 'hoppers would.

'Hoppers were not the only crawly visitors, for one summer in the middle 30's; there was a plague of giant spiders. They, too, came through the sky, floating along on great clumps of webs carried by the wind. These were an especially formidable looking spider, as large as hazel nuts and with heavy yellow markings. They came in great numbers and could be seen against the sun floating along from heaven knows where they originated. This spider invasion was never noted or explained by anyone; they infested only a small area and thus had not caught the attention of "scientists." They did no special harm except to gross us out, surrounded by these huge crawly spiders.

There was another plague to batter the farmers: anthrax. Hundreds of cattle around the region were dying of anthrax. There was no way to dispose of the large numbers of dead animals except to burn them in the pastures and fields where they fell. There were columns of black smoke rising from these burning piers in every direction.

During the late summer and early fall, smoke from forest fires to the north in Canada and Northern Minnesota were a common feature of every year. The fires were huge and largely unchecked. They produced great volumes of smoke which clouded the sun and colored the air a yellowish-tannish gray. There were few complaints and people seemed to accept the smoke from forest fires as a dependable feature of "Fall" in those years. For some, the smell of wood smoke was a kind of tonic which they seemed to enjoy.

Russian thistles were especially heavy during the dry years of 1933–34. Their rolling legions made the prairie into a thing of motion during high winds. Many fences were blown down from pressure of the wind against the wall of thistles caught in the fence wire.

Cockleburs were another plant that prospered during the dry years and became common in disturbed soils. They receded along with the dry weather. Another invader during the dry 1930's was the yellow "rosin weed" or yellow gum weed as it was called. It became common in the grass pastures and so heavily infested in some areas that cattle had sticky yellow coatings of rosin halfway up their legs.

Another natural phenomenon which was fairly common in the 1930's were the mirages that appeared on the horizon in the early morning, looking to the west. Some of these were quite graphic and fascinating. One could see buildings, farmsteads, groves of trees, and other features of the landscape which no one had ever seen before and had no idea of their origin or location. They were visible in the early morning and lasted only until the sun was high enough to change the lighting. People liked to see them because of their mysterious and magical and unexplainable nature.

There were marked increases in numbers of some wild animals during the dry years of the 1930's. Most notable were the jackrabbits. There were thousands of jack rabbits – so many that large parties of hunters were formed and rabbit drives arranged by which a string of hunters would stretch out – spread a few yards apart and all would walk in a single direction, driving the rabbits ahead of them, toward hunters posted below. Great piles of dead rabbits could result from such hunts and there was even a time when bounties from ten to twenty-five cents each were paid for rabbits.

There were always large flocks of ducks and geese in migration but in the dry years they stopped only where there were ponds or lakes for rest areas. Prairie chickens were still common in the 1920's – equal to the rising populations of the imported ring-necked pheasants.

Less evident to many was an invasion of large numbers of Flickertail Gophers. They were especially evident in 1932 and 1933 but were present in some numbers for over a decade. Where they came from was not clear – or where they went, when they left the country in the wetter years following the drought. They seemed to prosper in dry weather and in short grass pastures, like prairie dogs.

These gophers were larger than the common striped gopher which is everywhere in the region. These gophers had plain, unmarked fur coats, tan in color, rather like a prairie dog – they even looked and behaved a little like prairie dogs. They received their name from their habit of rapidly flicking their tails up and down when they are poised for action, such as diving into their holes. With the flickertails came the burrowing owls, who could be accommodated in the larger holes dug by these gophers in the same way that the owls live with prairie dogs. The owls had the capacity to hover in place for long periods of time and their distinctive cries at sundown were a familiar evening sound in those early days.

On the night of July 20, 1936, a large barn on the John Goss farm, northeast of Vilas, burned in a spectacular fire. The building was so dry that it virtually exploded and was completely aflame in 15 minutes. The entire frame was standing and all burning at once. It was a dramatic sight. People gathered from the entire neighborhood but there was nothing they could do because the fire burned so fiercely. Goss lost four horses, all of his harnesses and horse equipment and a store of hay which was of great value, since it was scarce during the drought years.

Such losses and hardships were more than enough for some local people and they joined in the larger migration from all over the Northern Plains to California and Oregon, in the hope of finding jobs and income.

The Drought Years were a natural happening and it was an unhappy coincidence that they came at the same time as the economic hardships of the Great Depression, which was affecting the entire nation.

Above: A small Ash grove is a tattered wreck from drouth, hot winds and grasshoppers.

Left: Grasshoppers by the millions covered the landscape.

Below: Thistles wind-driven, pile up in a grove and a fence line.

THE GREAT DEPRESSION

The economic depression of the 1930's began pretty much with the stock market crash in October 1929. The panic spread across the country. Businesses and factories closed in all directions. Thousands of jobs were lost, and at that time there were no company severance programs, no pensions, and no government aid or relief programs. If one lost his job, he was lost indeed.

Coupled with the severe drought on the plains, hardships multiplied. In 1932, there was a rag-tag army of World War I veterans who banded together from around the nation and marched on Washington, D. C. to demand help from the government. They set up a tent village in the Capitol and were finally dispersed by government troops who drove them out of their tent city and out of town.

By March, 1933, most banks across the nation were closed during a national "Bank Holiday," because people were making a run on banks to withdraw money which the banks could not supply. In a 100 day-long special session, the U.S. Congress passed President Franklin D. Roosevelt's "New Deal," which included many new social programs to provide financial help and jobs to the people. New laws provided for the creation of the Works Progress Administration, which provided thousands of jobs across the nation. WPA workers were employed in a great variety of outdoor improvement projects, such as building roads, dams to create lakes, bridges, parks, public buildings and many other public works projects.

Also, on December 5, 1933, President Roosevelt succeeded in achieving the repeal of the 18th Amendment to the federal constitution. This allowed the manufacture and sale of alcoholic drinks with the new 21st Amendment.

Other major social programs followed. In 1935, the Social Security program was established to provide financial help to old and retired people. In 1938, the first minimum

Over 1,500 hobos rode on a single freight train.

Horses and oxen pull a sod-breaking plow.

Grain bundles are stacked to await the threshers.

A typical tar-papered claim shack.

110

wage law in the U.S. was passed, providing new security to low income people.

The effects of the stock market crash in 1929, the bank failures and closings in 1933, the Veterans March on Washington, and the brutal efforts of the federal government and the corporations to put down strikes by workers are well known. The results for the people in the Vilas region were very low incomes and very low prices. Farm prices were so low as to bring despair: grain sold for ten or twenty cents a bushel, if there was any to sell.

Cattle sold for 10 and 20 dollars each. Farmers sometimes dumped their milk in the fields in protest for prices so low they would ensure financial ruin. Farmers who endured crop failures had to borrow at the banks using their farms and property as security. And when continued failure and inability to pay their debts forced them to quit, some joined the marchers and drifters and seekers of work – the growing army of hobos who rode the rails over the nation.

Both the drought years and the depression ended unevenly with the end of the decade of the thirties and with the outbreak of the Second World War. The war brought a demand for action, created jobs and forced the nation into a different mood.

One of the most remarkable things about the hard times of the 1930's is that the people who remained in their homes or on their farms remember it as a time when people were in good spirits. It is often said by them: "yes, times were tough but everyone was in the same boat. We were all poor but we didn't feel beaten down because of it – we didn't feel poor!" It is common for persons old enough to remember those times to say that while they had little or no money, they were happy anyway. Everyone was in the same condition. Their holidays and weekends were spent in neighborly visiting, and community dinners and picnics, dances and other simple diversions that didn't require much or any money.

There was no tense striving or competition to "get ahead." People were much more relaxed and calm of spirit than is true now.

HOLIDAYS

MAY DAY

Eighty years ago, there was an observance of May Day which now has largely been forgotten. The main activity was carried on by the school kids. May Day was a kind of observation of the arrival of spring – with warm sunny days and greening grass, together with the custom of giving "May Baskets." May baskets were made mostly in the schools with the encouragement of teachers who seemed to view the project as a positive aid to promote creativity.

The baskets were made by cutting out patterns of heavy bright colored construction paper and decorating them with cut-out designs and by gluing on a paper handle bowing over the top. They were about four to six inches square and about three inches deep. Often, they were lined with white or colored tissue paper.

May baskets were sometimes filled with candy and nuts but the more highly prized ones were filled with freshly picked flowers that bloomed on the prairie.

In the native prairie grass west and north of the Vilas School at just the end of April and early May, there were large patches of flowers that were called "daisies." Some were a bright white and others a deep blue – a cross between navy blue and cobalt. They had yellow centers and the blossoms were about an inch across; the plants grew about four or five inches high nestled in the grama grasses. Some of the flowers evidently were crossed between the blue and white and were a kind of rose-pink and much sought after for their rarity.

Another small flower that grew in the grass, low to the ground, was called the "salt and pepper flower" for it had a blossom with a background of off-white with little specks of black. In the spring also were the wild onions which one could dig out with a pocket knife, and skinning off the outer husk skins, eat on the spot. They gave the eater a powerful "onion breath."

There were many other flowers in that little prairie at other times of the summer: large scatterings of yellow coneflowers, and thick patches of pussytoes. Scattered everywhere were hills of buffalo beans with large fleshy beans the size of a hazel nut. Orange wild geraniums and many more wild flowers grew there as the months of summer passed by.

For May baskets, the flowers of choice were the blue and white "daisies" which were arranged in the little baskets and delivered before they could wilt, to the boys and girls who especially liked each other. A May basket was a token of affection. In delivering the baskets, it was intended that the giver should sneak up and place them on the doorstep of the admired one and get away without being caught. Thus, the pleased recipient was left to guess who might be the admirer. A custom so simple and quaint helps to define an era which is so far removed from the present.

THE FOURTH OF JULY

The Fourth of July seemed to have a special meaning to people before the Second World War. It was a day that appealed to everyone. While most everyone was vaguely aware of the anniversary of the nation's independence from England, freedom meant just that: Freedom! Freedom to do and be as you wanted to. It was a day of freedom from work – no one worked on the Fourth of July. It was a day for relaxation and visiting and eating and, for many, baseball and fire works and ice cream and family picnics.

In the 1920's, American had just won the first world war to make the nation safe for democracy and there was a strong streak of patriotism still abroad. Quite often the day was celebrated with a patriotic program – held outdoors, centered around a platform or band shell. There the politically powerful and the ambitious would catalog the array of human virtues and especially hard work, frugality, loyalty, honor to the forefathers, and similar themes. Often, too, the event included food – dishes brought by each family to share on common tables – potato salad, fried chicken, coleslaw, pickles and relishes, meat balls, sliced ham and beef, cakes and pies, and nearly endless other bounty, washed down with lemonade and coffee.

Often, the same pattern was followed in family gatherings and reunions. A bountiful table – potato salad and deviled eggs et all – but with several varieties of cakes with rich frostings and pies, and wonder of all – ice cream!

The ice cream was home made mixture of a rich custard of real cream, sugar and vanilla flavoring. This was put in a metal container which had a loose metal column with paddle-like flippers projecting from the sides. This metal canister filled with custard would be set down in a wooden tub, with cracked ice packed around it. A metal bar was fitted across the top of the tub and a small gear-box in the center was attached to the movable paddle inside the metal container. A hand crank turned the gears and the metal flippers inside the ice cream container. It became the job of the most eager and sturdy boys on hand to turn the crank for some time, until the cream inside became frozen solid and transformed into the miracle food. Then, typically, the ice cream freezer was covered with damp gunnysacks to insulate the ice and keep it from melting until it was time to eat. Waiting to eat it wasn't easy.

When the freezer was opened and the ice cream dished up there was never enough. Almost everyone loved it and would have been able to eat two or three times the amount given. Perhaps that was part of its endless appeal: one had to stop eating because it was gone – not because he had had enough! Large pieces of chocolate cake with caramel frosting helped to ease the pain, but there was never enough.

The center piece of every Fourth was the fireworks. Like other features of modern holidays, fireworks have changed since 1925. Then, there were no large year-round superstores. Fireworks were bought in small roadside stands and in the same general stores that sold everything else.

The fireworks were different from those sold now. Then, firecrackers were really firecrackers. While there were tiny ones called lady-fingers (about an inch long) that would go off with a refined "pop," the ones most prized were about four or five inches long and were called "cannon crackers." They really packed a wallop: it was common to put one under a large tin can and light it and step back. The can would blow 30 or 40 feet in the air with its bottom rounded out from the concussion. These big crackers were a challenge to the imagination. They could be set down in holes in wooden boards, to blow them apart. One could set them under slabs of rock or wood and blow that up. One could set them on the top of fence posts or light them and drop them into a well or cistern creating a resounding boom. The more enterprising would even tie smaller firecrackers – perhaps two inches long - to rocks, set them in a sling-shot – light the fuse and quickly shoot and thus create an "aerial bomb!"

Some older young men would arrange for more serious explosions. They set off dynamite at the crack of dawn to wake up the neighborhood with a bang on the Fourth of July.

There were other fireworks. One was a round, yellowish ball about the size of a small ping-pong ball that was filled

Prior to 1940, lakes were important recreational resorts for fishing, swimming, boating and picnics on the grassy shores.

with powder and which would explode when thrown against a hard surface – as a cement wall or a sidewalk. There were rockets, a larger version of the present bottle-rocket – a true sky rocket. There were smoke bombs and sparklers.

Toy pistols and revolvers were very popular with young kids because they were designed to shoot "caps." One could buy a package of rolls of red paper tape, in which tiny pockets of gun powder were spaced about an inch or so apart. The guns had a spring mechanism which would advance the tape and cause a hammer to fall on a patch of powder, by pulling the trigger. They made a sharp bang and were an endless delight for small boys playing cowboys and Indians – or, right after World War I, fighting imaginary enemies of our native land. Various designs for crude cannons were made out of old metal pipes or eave spouts, which were loaded with small stones to be shot off with big firecrackers, set in the breech.

There were endless variations of experiments, blowing up tin cans of all sizes, mainly for the awe of watching them sail skyward and come down with their ruptured or blown-out bottoms. Firecrackers were tied to the base of large weeds like sunflowers in attempts to blow them down.

Some families would go to a nearby lake for a family picnic and/or fishing party. Some would picnic at home or in a nearby grove of trees; there was no air conditioning anywhere, so the cool shade of a grove of trees was welcome. There were usually baseball games in the villages, with the locals vowing to humiliate the rowdy and villainous invaders.

In the evening, there were dances all around the area. Far less an occasion than the Fourth of July was needed to schedule a community dance. Sponsors were assured of a good turn out.

Fireworks displays were put on by local commercial and booster clubs, but they were small potatoes compared to the extravaganzas common today. Now, people tend to enjoy their fireworks vicariously – they watch instead of do. Technology has changed fireworks, too, much as it has every other feature of rural life. The huge rockets that are fired from banks of mortar barrels today, to lace the sky with streaks and shimmers of colorful fire didn't exist in 1920 Miner County. A part of the new pattern is a growing concern for safety and fear of injury. There were fewer grass fires – and buildings – lost to fires caused by careless and reckless shooting.

Parents today would be scandalized by the prospect of their seven year old kid being allowed to go off with his pals and a sackful of cannon crackers! Perhaps it is for the better – certainly there are fewer kids with fingers blown off and other serious injuries. But there is something lost as well and that has to do with what the Fourth of July was partly about: independence of spirit, self-reliance, courage, resourcefulness, and self-confidence.

HALLOWEEN HORROR

The night of October 31, 1930 was clear, crisp and still. It was Halloween and there was a huge orange harvest moon of the sort that the dark silhouettes of witches ride across on their broomsticks. A group of young men in their late teens and early twenties were abroad in the town bent on mischief, to do the pranks that had become the custom on Halloween night in the small prairie towns of that era.

Examples of the pranks they performed in Vilas on that night will represent the range of nuisance they could create: they painted Chris Larson's cow green; they placed small chairs and padlocks on residents' front yard gates; whitewash faces and mysterious markings were painted on the windows of nearly every home in town; they moved planters onto porches and blocked doorways with lawn furniture.

Their ingenuity was boundless. Above all, it was routine that they tip over every outhouse in town. Some citizens would sit up through the early part of the night while the marauders were abroad to protect this important installation.

Behind the Vilas blacksmith shop were living quarters for the smith and his family on the south side of the building. The grounds were surrounded by old, gnarled boxelder trees and in the backyard was an old wooden outhouse.

Upon reaching the center of the village, the band of young vandals turned down the dark side street along the west side of the blacksmith shop. They dashed over and tipped over the outhouse. The blacksmith, apparently having been on guard, stepped out from the shadows near his back door and fired a gun at the retreating band of boys. He hit one of them, Milo Wilson, in the head, killing him. The town was stunned and in an immediate uproar. The county sheriff was called; he arrested the blacksmith and took him to jail in Howard.

Over several ensuing days, a search was conducted for the murder weapon, to no avail. On the third or fourth day of the search the gun was found. It was a .32 caliber revolver. It had been hidden under a sheet of tin, nailed high in the board roof of the blacksmith shop.

The blacksmith was tried and found guilty of manslaughter and was sentenced to twelve and a half years in the South Dakota State Penitentiary.

Villagers who knew the blacksmith, whose name was Anton Benesh, described him as a quiet, moody, dour man who kept to himself and had a gloomy personality. Someone professed to having heard him say, prior to the shooting, that if anyone tried to damage his property on Halloween night, they would suffer for it.

The murder of Halloween night in 1930 was the basis of gossip and recollection on Halloweens for years following the event, until almost everyone who remembered it had died or moved away.

THANKSGIVING

In 1920, Thanksgiving Day meant large family dinners, in the best Norman Rockwell tradition, with a large turkey as the centerpiece. In the 20's and 30's Thanksgiving followed a fairly established pattern every year. As an example, our family and some friends, all in their Sunday best, would gather at noon, around a table with a huge roasted turkey stuffed with dressing and gizzards, mashed potatoes and gravy, green beans, pickles, homemade bread and rolls, jello salads, apple, mince and pumpkin pies, various cookies and cakes. All of the ladies would bring foods and they would all bustle around for several hours setting the table and arranging all of the goodies.

The men would all gather in the living room and talk of the weather, of farm crops, of politics or wherever fancy led them until dinner was announced. Dinner itself was a ritual of one to two hours during which everyone ate all they could hold, after which the women would wash the dishes and the men would retire to the living room, where they would light cigars and begin a game of whist which would continue into the evening. The room and the entire first floor would be so filled with cigar smoke that the air was heavy and blue. The cigars were likely the "White Owl" brand and came in wooden boxes which were prized as containers for small items when empty. Cigar and pipe smoking was common among adult men; cigarettes were not widely used until the early and middle 30's.

The ladies would sit around the dining table and drink coffee and visit. The kids were busy playing board games, hide and seek and other games around the house. As late afternoon approached, they again set out a table with leftovers from the turkey feast but with a heavy emphasis on desserts such as cakes, cookies and pie. When the sun had gone down and dark was approaching, folks would gather up their coats and the day would be over with everyone tired and happy.

A large part of such occasions was simply the enjoyment of each other's company and the chance to "visit." Such happenings were a large factor in building community and keeping harmony among the neighbors.

CHRISTMAS

Christmas as a holiday and as a season has evolved substantially since 1920 in Miner County. Seventy or eighty years ago, Christmas was a much more simple, less gilded experience. Public decoration of streets, public buildings and homes had yet to become a mania and evolved gradually with the access to electricity and invention of plastic devices, colored lighting and the like. Christmas decoration in those early times was largely confined to the interior of the home.

Christmas shopping as known today did not exist, either in the intensity of promotion or in the profusion of items produced specifically to be sold as Christmas gifts. Christmas had not yet become commercialized as a major feature of the retail year.

The Christmas trees were nearly always natural green spruce trees, set in the parlor or family room. They were decorated with homemade strings of popcorn and long strings of fresh cranberries threaded on cotton grocer's string. Glittery tin-foil tinsel, cut in long thin strings, were draped over the ends of the spruce branches. Angels or a stars decorated the tops of the trees. And there were candles – real wax candles, about four inches long and a half inch in diameter, which were set in little tin candle holders with spring clamps on their bottom, to attach them to the tree branches.

When the family or public group was assembled in the school or church, these candles were lit and gave out a warm yellowish glow as candles do. They were actually burning

– often a dozen or a score or more on a single tree. The fire hazard this presented is unthinkable today. The trees were highly flammable and should a single candle tip over it could quickly ignite the tree needles and the entire tree could explode quickly into flame. Thus, the candles had to be watched carefully and immediate measures were taken if needed. Occasionally, it would happen that a tree would catch on fire but rarely, with disastrous outcomes.

Other Christmas decorations were mainly of evergreen boughs, red ribbons, pine cones and glass balls, for table centerpieces and about the home. Evergreen wreaths were more commonly attached to doors and on windows.

The Christmas dinner was a festive affair and according to family tradition would have been held on Christmas Eve or at midday on Christmas Day. If on Christmas Eve, it was an occasion for large kettles of oyster stew with crackers. Christmas Day dinners featured a variety of meat dishes, – goose, pheasant, chicken, pork or beef roast and almost certainly, mashed potatoes and gravy and home-canned vegetables. In some cases, this menu was supplemented by ethnic dishes, such as lutefisk, pickled herring and lefse and a profusion of pastries, wursts, or sausages, pork, boiled potatoes, cabbage, turnips and parsnips and breads and pastries. There might have been dumplings, with meats, in a variety of dishes. Desserts always included fruit pies, such as apple, cherry, rhubarb and often, mince pies. There would be cakes and cookies of great variety.

Christmas goodies consisted of nuts in the shell, hard candies, peanut brittle, and fresh fruits such as apples and oranges, which might serve as stocking stuffers for children.

The activities in the home kitchen produced a good deal of heat and steam which created remarkable patterns of frost on the window panes to attract the interest of the children, to wonder at the infinite tracery of patterns and to draw their own additions in the frost with finger nails.

Christmas gifts in those years tended to be of a practical nature and commonly consisted of items of clothing, sometimes made by the women of the family such as knitted mittens, caps or scarves. Often clothing items were ordered in advance from mail order companies, such as Sears, Roebuck or Montgomery Ward and hidden away in trunks and closets, to be brought out and put under the Christmas tree. If the family could afford it, there might be clamp-on ice skates, steel runner sleds, coaster wagon, bicycles, or spring-driven mechanical toys for the children.

Weather in the Christmas season in those years was generally more cold and severe than in more recent times, and travel through deep snow and against icy winds was daunting. But people dressed warmly and spirits were generally light and cheerful.

Family members tended to live in closer proximity to each other than is now true. Most people were farmers or small town retailers or service workers. Youth tended to remain in the community and work on the family farm and to stay, marry and remain there. So, Christmas gatherings quite often would attract a substantial number of clansmen, kids, aunts, uncles and cousins.

There were few public events to draw people away from the home. Travel to warmer, holiday "getaways" was largely unknown, and would have been impractical for most people.

People traveled in sleighs and buggies with snow runners in heavy winters. They bundled up under great robes of buffalo and horsehides, woolen blankets and heavy home-sewn patch-work quilts. Sleigh bells were often attached to the horse's harness and jingled as they moved along. In many ways, the horse-drawn conveyances were more reliable and far less demanding than the early autos that gradually replaced them. In the 20's and 30's, while the driver of the sleigh had to harness and take care of the horses both coming and going, the auto driver was faced with terrible difficulties in cranking (by hand) car engines in which oil and grease was nearly solid from the cold and where radiators were frozen if not drained – and filled again with teakettles of boiling water from the kitchen stoves – and batteries that may have failed from the cold.

In and around Vilas, in the county, community Christmas programs usually followed a pattern. Programs held in the schools and churches often included a community elder or a clergyman who read the accounts of Christ's birth from the King James Bible. A children's program presented a tableau of the Nativity scene, and choruses of the youngest kids sang old favorites like "Silent Night." Music was from a piano or a foot pumped parlor organ. At the end of it all, there would be a distribution of candies, nuts, and cookies to everyone present, especially the children. There would be a natural Christmas tree – larger than those in private homes – but also covered with live, burning candles and other decorations usually home made. Interior lighting would be provided by a profusion of burning candles.

Religious services in the area churches were common. The people of the region at that time were mostly entirely conservative Christians. If people attended church at all, it would have been in a main-line Christian congregation. There were no people of color of any description living in those rural communities at that time.

In the 1920's and 30's, the Christmas season had far less of an emphasis on commercialism. There was far less pressure in the public media to buy presents, hold company parties, take expensive holiday trips and the welter of promotions now common. It was less shrill, tense and driven than now seems true. Now one might wish for a gift of the serenity and peace that was abroad in that earlier time.

Of all the holidays, Christmas was the most universally loved and observed. It really was a time of peace and good will and was probably the most cherished memories of many families of that era.

WINTER PLAY FOR KIDS

Winter in the 20's and 30's almost certainly meant snow and storms. Nowadays, nearly every heavy snow is described as a blizzard but it shouldn't be: it is simply a heavy snow. A blizzard is a storm in a class by itself: bitter cold, well below zero; savage winds above 30 miles an hour; dark, leaden skies and heavy snow driven by the wind. Blizzard snow is fine snow, nearly like a powder. This is no snow with big fat fluffy flakes slowly wafting down. Blizzard snow is more like a swirling cloud of frozen flour, driven by the wind, reaching in every crack and crevice around a door or window. It gives new meaning to the expression "white-out" for one really cannot see any distance ahead of himself and in the dark, all directions seem the same.

There were not many storms like this then, but there were some. The wind drove the snow into high drifts and filled the ditches, creek beds and depressions of any kind. It would pile in great drifts and the severe cold would freeze the drifts so hard one could walk over the tops of them. Cattle and farm animals were known to escape their pens and pastures by walking over the tops of the fences buried below in the drifts.

These hard snow drifts were great for kids to play on, to slide down on steel runner sleds and to dig out caves and tunnels in and under them. Kids found that they could build wonderful igloos, by cutting blocks of the hard snow with an old carpenter's rip saw. They would cut the blocks and stack them up in a constantly narrowing circle until there was only a small hole in the top of the igloo's dome. They would trim off the rough corners with the saw, cut a clean, round-topped hole for a door, and build a short tunnel to the door. Inside, they would trim and smooth down the rough spots in the wall. Then, they would build a small bonfire in the center under the small hole in the roof. The smoke would rise like it was supposed to, out the hole, and, wonder of wonders, the heat inside melted the inner surface of the walls, which would in turn, freeze and form a smooth surface of ice on the walls, which was absolutely wind proof! It was warm inside those igloos. One could take off his heavy coat and sit cross-legged around the fire like many primitive savages must have done, over thousands of years before.

The old wood saws were a wonderful aid in much snow construction of stairs, tunnels and forts and walls of great variety. Kids built conventional snowmen and conducted snowball fights, which sometimes took on the character of ongoing wars, lasting several days. Great piles of snowballs were made up in advance. The practice of soaking snowballs in water and then freezing them into ice balls was considered unfair though it was done, as was the placing of ice cubes or even rocks or bits of coal inside the snowball, to give it great weight and speed.

Sleds were used mainly for down-hill sliding, which meant a long trudge back up to the top again for another exciting swoop down the slope. Sleds had practical uses, too, for hauling stuff around the yard, in doing chores or even of going to the store and bringing home a load of groceries. Sleds varied greatly in size, to hold one or two small kids, on up to long ones that could hold four or five. Homemade ones had runners of wood, with a strip of steel edging screwed to the bottom of the runner. Such steel-faced runners were sometimes fixed under wooden boxes to make a sort of "freight" sled. Finally, there were the sleighs and sleds drawn by one or more horses. These were like farm wagons with runners instead of wheels. There were bobsleds, buggies with runners and a variety of the larger ones. These larger sleighs and sleds were often the major means of conveyance for families to visit the neighbors, attend church, and go to do their "trading."

Kids had a number of games to be played in the snow. Probably the most common was "Fox and Goose," in which a large circle was stepped off in the fresh snow to form the circle. Paths were made inside it to form a cross, from the center of the circle out to the edges. One kid would be chosen to begin as "Fox." His job was to chase the other kids around the circle and up and down the paths until he was able to catch and tag one, who then became the Fox, repeating the process until all were exhausted or tired of it all.

Ice skating was popular and nearly all kids had ice skates. These were amazingly primitive by current standards. Shoe skates were unknown to kids of that era. Their skates were made of steel with a flat platform that fit against the sole of one's shoe or boot. Steel clamps that fitted over the edge of the sole of the shoe were tightened with a metal key which screwed the clamps tighter and tighter until they were firmly fixed to the bottom of the shoe. Then, for extra security, there were light leather straps that buckled around over the shoes to insure a tighter fit. Kids' winter shoes and boots were generally strong and heavy, intended for rough usage. There were games called "hockey" played with whatever rules the kids could cook up on a given occasion. The hockey sticks were just that – sticks – and the puck was any small item suitable – perhaps a tin can or a block of wood.

Skiing was far less common since no one owned "real" skis and most had never seen them. So the skis were homemade, too, from wooden barrel staves which were slightly curved up at the ends and were smooth enough to serve on the bottom side. Leather straps held the shoes fixed to the center of the stave. With the rounded side down and when strapped on, the skier could slide down hills or slide behind a sleigh or buggy hanging on with a rope. They were clumsy, didn't work very well and were hard to keep fastened onto one's shoes, so they were not in wide use.

For kids living on farms with barns large enough to have a haymow (most all of them did) it was possible to have fun rolling around and jumping into piles of prairie hay. It was warmer than outdoors and it was possible to tunnel in and under piles of hay, in games of a form of hide and seek.

In general, winter play meant outdoor activity for there were far fewer diversions available for kids indoors in those times. And, they were encouraged to go outside by their mothers on the reasoning that exercise was good for them and made them more easy to handle.

All of these activities were adequate to produce kids with cheeks as rosy as apples and bright eyes and happy with the inventiveness required to do it all. There were few instances where any adult had any part or was even present in any of these doings. The kids did it all themselves, making their own rules and constructing their own solutions to getting it all done.

THE PRAIRIE IN MINER COUNTY

THE NATURAL PRAIRIE

Geology can tell us a great deal about the ancient past in Miner County. The county is a square which contains 571 square miles. It is generally flat country, with low rolling hills, which lay between the Vermillion Hills to the east and the James River to the west. The altitude is about 1350 – 1400 feet. The county has a natural divide down the middle, north to south. In the eastern half, the natural flow of water is toward the Vermillion River. In the western half, water flows toward the James River.

There are differences in the amount of rainfall, too. The western half is often a little drier than the east. The soils vary, being darker and heavier on the east side to lighter and sandier in the west.

There are four major streams that flow south through the county: the west fork of the Vermillion River, Wolf Creek, Rock Creek, and Redstone Creek. All are intermittent streams except in the spring or in exceptionally wet years. All of them are the remains of ancient flow channels left by the melting glaciers, thousands of years ago.

Lakes and ponds come and go with available rain and snow melt. A dam at Carthage insures that waters in Redstone Creek are captured to create a very attractive small lake for campers, fisherman and nature students. The Twin Lakes south of Roswell are old lake beds that have gradually silted in and made very shallow lakes in wet years for water birds and bullheads. In dry years, they may get very low or disappear completely. During the 1930's, Artesian wells on

Central Miner County

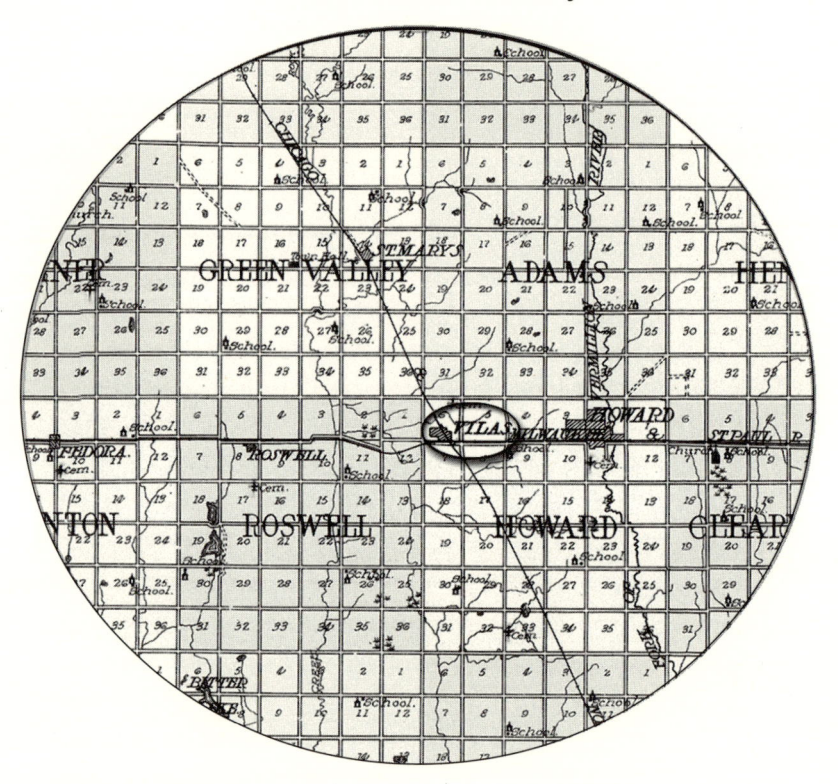

Miner County was created in 1873 by the Territorial Legislature and was named for Captain Nelson Miner, organizer of the 1st Dakota Cavalry and for Ephiram Miner, a prominent grain miller in Yankton. It was organized in 1880 and the present boundaries were established in 1883. The county is composed of 16 townships each containing 36 mile-square sections for a total of 527 square miles. The town of Vilas is located near the center of the county.

the south tip of the lakes poured in a great volume of water and filled the lake beds. All over the county there are many large ponds which attract water birds but which are dependent on surface water to fill them up. Together they are important in supporting the varied wild life of the area.

Before the white settlers came and claimed the land, the county was a wilderness of grass – many different kinds of grasses blended together. The tall native grasses – Big Blue Stem, Little Blue Stem, Switch and Indian grasses, all from three to six feet high – are largely gone now. However, they are gaining new foothold in some areas of the county under the Conservation Reserve Program of the U.S. Department of Agriculture. The tall native grasses are being replanted to cover areas where the soil is light and subject to erosion. These new grass fields make wonderful homes for the small prairie birds who live in this region and, of course, for the larger game birds like the ring-necked pheasant, the prairie chicken and grouse. The shorter native grasses are especially hardy and tolerant of heat and can withstand extended droughts, and dry times.

During the 1930's drought, many pastures were worn down to the dirt with little or no grass showing. But the dormant roots were alive and when the rains came again, the grasses revived and grew again. Among these is blue grama, often called buffalo grass, though it is really a different grass. Blue grama is often found on the driest hill tops and sunny slopes. It has a blueish-green color, grows from four to six inches tall. In late summer, the grass turns a light tan in color and becomes a curly thick natural carpet.

Other related grasses, like side oats grama, and green needle grass and others made up the natural grass carpet that overlaid the county. Among the most common native trees able to withstand the winds and dry weather were the cottonwood, ash, boxelder, white willow, cedar and plum.

There are lots of what are called weeds which grow up to some size, like the several sunflowers, ragweed, pigweed, and curly dock. They with others mix together with white sage and other aromatics to fill the air with a distinctive perfume after a summer rain. When the yellow and white clovers are in bloom, they completely fill the air, as will a patch of wild roses.

SLOUGHS AND WETLANDS

The people who lived on farms in small prairie towns like Vilas during the 20's and 30's, had a better opportunity than is now possible to become acquainted with the animals, birds and plants that made up the natural prairie. That was possible because a part of what we now call "wetlands" – the sloughs, reed-covered marshes, ponds and tiny creeks – have disappeared because they have been drained or farmed over.

The sloughs were the most common place to find natural surface water. Most were shallow depressions made by a receding glacier. The actions of wind and rain over the centuries since washed dirt into the low spots. This allowed reeds and heavy grasses to move in and to create shorelines and groups of dark green islands and open waterways over the face of the slough. They were a marvelous haven for all kinds of small animals, like frogs and toads, turtles, small snakes and lizards.

The sloughs were a natural home for the red-winged and yellow headed blackbirds. Many birds, including the larks and small birds of the prairie grasses would come by for a drink or a bath. The slough is the natural home for a legion of shore birds like the great blue heron, the smaller night heron and the American bittern – known to country people

Redwing Blackbirds dominate prairie wetlands.

Prairie Chickens are true Dakota natives, predating pheasants.

Photos by South Dakota Tourism

as the "Slough Pumper" because of its hoarse rasping, croaking call, like the noise of an old wooden hand pump.

Among the reeds and cattails, the blackbirds built their nests, woven to the heavy reed stalk. They were perfectly protected spots for the young birds, free of the wandering coyote or the barn cats from neighboring farms. Great number of ducks, coots, and griebes nested there also, with the same advantages. Little ducks could hide among the rushes and reeds from the eyes of passing hawks and owls. They could sleep in peace, protected from all the four-legged predators out looking for a midnight lunch.

To be near and see all of this close at hand was appealing. My older brother, Austin, conceived the idea of building our own small boat in which we could poke our way out into the reeds and see everything close at hand.

We scouted around for scrap lumber – boards and thin strips for battens. And we used some tar and hemp binder twine for caulking, to fill cracks and make it water-tight. We ended up with a crude but serviceable small boat with a flat bottom, flat sides and square ends, like a shallow shoe box, but it was watertight!

The boat had a seat with room for the two of us and with it we could paddle and pole ourselves around a big wetland, going among the channels of open water and exploring the slough to our heart's content. No one worried about us, because the water was only a couple of feet deep and if our boat sank, we could have walked out of the slough, anyway. As things were, it worked fine and we were proud of ourselves. We learned from building and using the primitive boat, which we poled slowly along the walls of cat-tails, watching the turtles that might come alongside, or looking into the nest of a red-wing blackbird.

Sloughs were the natural home of muskrats, who would build a winter house in the form of a pile of rushes and mud that would stick a foot or two above the waterline where they were protected from the weather. We spent hours watching the behavior of a dozen varieties of duck, swimming about, fighting over problems not clear to us and raising bunches of little ducklings that would swim around, following their parents in single-file.

Sitting quietly in the boat, we learned the sounds that rise up in sloughs, like the different noises that a single species of duck might make, depending on what it was doing. Just about all of the creatures make a variety of sounds, and we learned to recognize many of them and in doing so felt more at home with them.

In the spring evenings there would be an unending chorus of frogs. They could be heard a half a mile away on a quiet evening. Many of the sloughs that existed in 1920 are gone now, having been drained to allow the land to be grazed or farmed, causing an unintended loss of a source for ground water to replenish and the removal of places for the ducks and other water birds to live. The prairie is a less attractive place without them.

One of the memorable features of an established prairie slough is the particular smell it creates. It is a sweetish/musty combination of decaying reeds and cattails, scores of living plants and blossoms, together with mosses, algae and the countless other tiny plants and animals that live in or on the water. It is a unique smell that captures all of the life and activity of that special little community.

WILDFIRES

Among the most dramatic happenings on the prairie were the wildfires – the prairie fires. Today, it is hard to imagine the size of the area some of them covered. Rarely now, it is possible to see a small version of what the pioneers experienced.

Prairie fires were started by lightning strikes, until man came along with his bonfires for cooking, heating, smoking, signaling or whatever. Depending on the weather conditions of humidity, extended drought, wind and temperatures, the effects of such fires can vary greatly. Driven by a hot summer wind over a dry tall grass prairie, a fire can move with tremendous speed, since the wind will blow burning embers ahead of the main blaze and speed the forward progress. The wind increases the temperature too, making the fire into kind of a huge blow-torch. The main virtue of such fires is that they pass quickly if wind driven and burned-over areas cool fairly soon after its passage.

Since it would be nearly impossible to out-run such a fire, the lives of some folks have been saved from a large fire passing over them by getting down in a creek or pond or by going down into a "cyclone cellar" – a dugout pit with a timber and dirt roof over the top. A person on horseback could escape the smaller fires by riding off at a right angle to the edge of the approaching fire.

Most people are attracted to fires. We gather to watch a house or barn burn or any other large fire. In the early times, there were no regulations against the burning of trash or rubbish and it was common for people to burn weed patches, fence rows, ditches and sometimes entire fields of grass or stubble. Dry leaves and grass around the yard and house were raked up and ceremoniously burned in bonfires on still fall evenings. There is something hypnotic about watching the flames; rise and curl in such small fires, and, for many, the smell of burning leaves and dry twigs give a primal feeling of comfort and reassurance that all is right with the world.

In the great drought of the 1930's, among the hallmarks of the time was the abundance of Russian thistles that grew in the farm fields and in any patch of disturbed soil. They were everywhere and they prospered because they were suited to the dryness and heat and general climate conditions of the time. Russian thistles were often cut and used for forage for farm animals because there was virtually nothing else growing in the pastures or hay fields. The thistles grew into a sort of round ball when mature and gave new meaning to the term "tumble weed." They would break loose in the endless winds and roll across the field until they had created a ramp against the fence, which would permit the weeds that followed to roll up over the barrier against the fence and roll on to more distant barriers!

Farmers would burn thistles when they were dry in the fall, partly to keep them from building up on the fences. Thistles scattered seeds along the way as they rolled along – a very effective seeding system of Ma Nature!

Burning thistles presented a new challenge to rural burners: one had to burn at times when the wind was down or the burning thistles might set off a new kinds of prairie fire, since they could roll along for some distance, while burning, from the fire site. The story is told of a farmer, north of Vilas, who set out to burn a field of thistles and had no more than begun when a wind came up and started blowing burning thistles directly toward his straw pile and farm buildings! He ran about frantically beating down the rolling, burning thistles with his pitchfork to keep them from starting a larger fire that he could not contain. He barely succeeded and saved the day; his epic fight became a story which neighbors repeated to warn each other.

Efforts to fight grass fires in the early times were limited by the means available. These were usually barrels of water hastily loaded onto farm wagons – and wet gunny sacks soaked in the water barrels which were used to beat down the flames, with the help of rakes, hoes and forks.

Farmers whose buildings adjoined fields of stubble or grass which could burn if a fire started, often plowed fire breaks between the buildings and the field. In a high wind they were of limited help, for the fire blew burning embers across the plowed ground. A fire break helped if the grass or stubble was short and the wind was low.

Prairie fires were a serious hazard. An old man told an account of a happening that occurred years before. He said a man was walking across the prairie toward a store where he could buy a sack of flour to take home. He saw a large prairie fire rising up ahead of him but fortunately for him, the wind would carry it to the side and past him. He continued walking and soon was in the burned over area, which was still smoldering with the remains of the stalks of plants and of buffalo chips. Soon he came upon a sod hut and the smoking ruin of a straw shed/shelter for the animals. He walked up to it and upon coming around to the front side, found a young woman huddled on a large rock, sobbing with two small children with her. Hearing him approach, she looked up. He said he would never forget her face covered dark with ashes from the fire and white streaks where the tears had run down her face! He tried to comfort her with little success and he walked on, to the store. When he returned, he again passed the sod hut but it was deserted then and he never learned what happened to the woman and children.

EARLY ROADS

Roads around Vilas and Miner County have followed the same evolution as the rest of the society. They began simply as trails across the grass – the "two-track" made by wagon wheels. Before that they were one-tracks – cow paths and game trails. When the first settlers came they followed the trails which were pretty wide. Covered wagons and stage coaches followed a trail but when the ruts got too deep or too muddy, they moved over a notch and made a second trail beside the first. The next wave might move over still farther and after a while there could be a trail a half a mile wide – a trail very hard to miss.

When the land surveys laid out the county and township road rights-of-way, leaving a band of land between the sections for a public road, they became two-tracks at first and when there were enough people and traffic, someone decided they should be graded, with a ditch to drain off the rain water. This helped to build dry roads and enabled a road grader to smooth out the bumps and fill in the mud holes. In the 1920's and 30's, mud holes were a well known reality on the township roads. Today most roads in general use are graveled, but then they were simply dirt and low spots had to have culverts and drainage ditches to make them passable.

Anyone who has never driven down a dirt road in a model T Ford after several days rain has no understanding of what travel was like for our grandfathers. The cars did not have much power, first of all – the wheels would sink down in the wet mud and would pull the car to a stop when one hit a true mud hole. The driver might try to find some weeds or brush along the road to put under the tires to give them more traction.

Passengers might get out and push. But it's hard to push when you have to wade around in the mud. And, sometimes you really were stuck. What to do? Go for help, probably, to the nearest farm house in hope the farmer would bring a team of horses and pull you out. And even if you found the farmer at home and he was willing to come, it meant quite a delay for he would have to get his horses, harness them, to hitch on to the car, so the horses could pull it. And even if all of that went well, it was still no joke to keep the car moving ahead, for there would be other mud holes on up the line.

Getting over the dirt roads in the warm months of the year could often be trying but it could get just plain tough in winter. The early cars were not the best for plowing through

Mechanical ditch diggers speeded road building, replacing horses with pulling scoops called fresnos.

Steam engines provided power for many large machines.

An early Model T Ford had cloth side curtains and celluloid windows.

snow drifts. They would get stuck and the driver and passengers would have to get out and shovel and push to get moving again. Sometimes, again the last resort was to appeal to the nearest farmer for help.

The cars were cold and drafty, besides. They had no heaters and the early ones had only side curtains of cloth with celluloid windows. If your feet got cold riding along, there wasn't much that could be done to help you. Riders in the cars in winter had to bundle up with blankets, quilts and robes of horse hide and buffalo, with the hair still on them to stave off the cold.

Gradually, everything improved to allow better road maintenance and greater speed. And as things progressed, a few of the main roads were surfaced with asphalt, which made them seem like heaven, compared to the old, dirty, bumpy ones. The cars finally got heaters that worked and kept one warm and they went much faster.

In bitter, freezing weather, drivers had to drain the water out of their radiator to keep it from freezing. When they were ready to go again, they would take teakettles of boiling water and rush out to fill the radiator before the engine overheated. Sometimes, the car wouldn't start anyway, and they would have to go through the process again, before they could go anywhere.

In the early years, people would use the old soapstone foot heaters that had been used in the horse-drawn buggies. These were slabs of a soft stone that held heat well and which were heated in the oven of a cook stove; then wrapped in a heavy towel or blanket to hold in the heat, they were placed on the floor of the car.

The early cars offered other hazards. There was no decent antifreeze except alcohol to put in the auto radiators. Without alcohol and sometimes with it, they froze up and the engine would overheat and stall. The batteries were much less reliable and less able to withstand deep cold. In tough weather, they might fail and there was no power to start the engine. The motor oil was not well adapted to handle cold and it would get heavy and stiff, making it hard to turn over the engine. There were instances where the car owner would drain the engine oil out before leaving the car out in the cold and take it in the house. Before he was ready to leave again, he would set the oil on the stove to warm it up before putting it back into the engine. Problem was, unless the oil was carefully watched, it would overheat and boil over unto the stove and start a fire in the house. Sometimes a house would burn down as a result of careless handling of the oil in cold weather.

Frost on the windshield was a problem for there were no warm air blowers in the car to blow the frost away. Windshields frosted over from the breath of the people in the car and the driver had to stop and scrape the windshield clear enough to see to drive.

Taken together, the hazards of travel which seem quaint and hard to believe now were commonplace in the 20's and 30's.

CRICKET – CHIRPING NIGHTS

In 1920 and 1930 in rural Miner County, it was very quiet on summer nights. On the prairie in summer, the wind almost always goes down with the sun and comes up with the sun. In those times, there was an almost complete lack of noise from engines, motors, aircraft and all-night semis on the highways. Those things did not yet exist, for the most part. True, it is still pretty quiet away from the towns at night, but then, there was almost a complete absence of noise.

Generally speaking, noise pollution comes from having a growing technology and more and more people, just as air pollution does. Fewer people equals less pollution in almost every way. Miner County – and Vilas – had many more people in 1920 than it has now but it has a much higher level of technology – more tractors and big farm machines with engines which helps make up the difference.

There was far less light pollution then, too. The only lights to be seen looking across the countryside were a couple of dim, yellowish lights from kerosene lamps in nearby farmhouses. There were no electric lights anywhere, except in the distant towns. The only lights in the farm yard came from kerosene barn lanterns.

Almost everyone realized that the moon and stars are brighter and seem more real, away from artificial lights. There were no car radios, let alone boom-boxes to rend the peace. Loud speakers and amplifiers of all kinds were all in the future. When lack of light and sound are combined the word quiet takes on new meaning. One is forced to look out and away from himself since he is no longer insulated by the illusion of the presence of others. There is nothing to insulate one from the reality of nature. Such noises as one would hear at night were the noises of the chirping of crickets, maybe the cry of a night bird or the barking of a distant dog or coyote.

In Miner County, one certain night sound was the long-drawn whistle of the railroad freight trains, a kind of mournful reassuring sound that the outer world was hanging together and working as it should.

Such a setting makes a mark on people who experience it. One is compelled to sense that nature – the creation – is a very large and complex place and that the light and noise that man creates can divert him from the realizations that he has a modest role in it all.

The stars were especially impressive, and the Milky Way was a reality! So many stars and clusters of bodies together that it seemed like a great wide band of lighted gases or fog. And, the moon is never so orange as when it first rises in full on a summer night. Scientists may tell us that the bright orange color and the size are all illusions created by dust in the air and refraction of light. But that doesn't really destroy the magic of a full harvest moon. Now, there are satellites zooming back and forth; then, the only moving objects were meteors. A common pastime in the early evening was to lie on the grass and count the number of meteor streaks in a time period.

Close association with the large forces of nature had the effect of placing one more in harmony with nature's schedule and clockwork. One was a part of the natural calendar – sowing and gathering into barns. Now a more artificial man-made environment seeks to even out the seasons to make us cooler in summer and warmer in winter and to create an atmosphere in which we feel we are in control: nature is subject to our whims and resources to modify it.

One is led to wonder whether our efforts to speed things up – to get more done in less time – to light the workplace, to extend the day – to heat and cool the setting, to extend the season – tend to take us out of harmony with the timetables of nature and that pressing harder constantly leads to an understandable level of stress in people – which we also try to modify by gulping handfuls of over-the-counter pills to calm our uneasiness.

Thus does the quiet summer night lead us to reflections that can change our view of how things operate and how we change?

THE CYCLONES OF SUMMER

Anyone who grew up in central Miner County knows about wind – how the wind blows almost every day of the year, mostly from the northwest in winter and the southwest in summer. When it blows from the southeast, it is likely to help blow up a rain – if it rains at all. A wind from the northeast will almost certainly bring rain – if it rains at all!

In the 1930's spring and summer storms seemed nearly always to come from the southwest. The big, dramatic storms in spring almost always came in June. They would begin with a gradual darkening of the sky in the southwest – dark blue and darker purple. Thunderstorms usually formed quickly and the worst of them would have the most dramatic sky: huge cumulus clouds, wispy, swirling clouds, sometimes clouds made up of a field of round small bumpy ones, reminiscent of a herd of sheep. When the storm was near and about to break, the clouds overhead were awesome and hard to describe – deep, dark bluish-greenish gray, whirling twisting, shooting in erratic directions: it was clear to almost anyone looking up that they were going to get pounded.

Getting pounded meant a hail storm – ice of varying sizes. Some storms would bring ice in jagged chunks, some reported as large as golf balls and some like baseballs and some even as large as grapefruit.

Depending on the size of the hail and the length of time it came down and the strength of the wind driving it, hail storms can do enormous damage to farm crops. In terrible ice storms, the field crops can be pounded into the ground with little or nothing left standing in the field, which before the storm, gave promise of a bountiful crop. Large ice chunks can ruin buildings, too, pounding holes in the roofs, smashing out windows, and killing unprotected animals.

There was an account of one storm so severe that it pounded even grass pastures so they looked like dirt fields and which blasted off the gray coating of erosion of fence posts so they shone bright like new wooden posts!

Cyclones – as tornadoes were called in those days – were common in the 30's. They were especially bad ones in 1934 and 1936, and like most notable summer storms in the area, occurred in late June.

Many farmers and some town dwellers had "cyclone cellars" – an underground shelter dug out and covered with a board roof and a mound of earth, with a stairway going down into it. There may have been a board floor and benches built around the walls for people to sit on, to wait out the tempest raging over their heads.

Stories were legion of freak happenings caused by the winds of cyclones. On one occasion, straws from a straw pile were carried by winds with such force they were driven into the trunks of ash trees and stuck out like thorns or quills. Ash trees are a relatively hard wood and for straws to be driven into them like nails is a remarkable thing. Another time, an iron cistern pump and pipe were pulled up out of a cistern and laid out on the ground a short distance away, with no harm done to the cover of the cistern – or the pump. Some years ago, the story was told of an old man in Roswell, who was tending a small gas station along Highway #34, when a storm blew up. It came along and lifted the gas station up and away, over his head; he was left sitting on his chair on the bare cement floor – all that remained of the gas station!

The rain that came along with the storm might come in huge, heavy drops that went "splat" when they hit. Or maybe in a fine mist, driven by very high winds. There would almost always be some huge, high-powered lightning bolts and hair raising thunder claps along with the tempest.

After a June storm was over, and was faintly rumbling off to the east, the wonderful fresh smell in the air seemed to make it all worthwhile. The air washed clean of dust, the smell of many prairie flowers, plants and grasses soaked by the rain the smell of the wet prairie earth itself all blended together to make a unique and memorable smell.

The low spots, sloughs and ditches were filled with fresh clean water for a short time. In really heavy rains, some of the larger sloughs might gain enough water to remain through much of the summer. But in the end, almost all of the new

Tornadoes were called cyclones in the early years; funnels like this one in 1929 were fairly common.

Behind Chris Larsen, Vilas' mail carrier, is the wooden foot bridge, the church and the school house.

Railroad snow plows try to clear the tracks of huge drifts.

water soaked away or was taken up by the sun and the endless prairie winds.

At various points in South Dakota, there are what the locals call "tornado alleys" or "hail alleys," or some such title. These are pathways on the landscape running southwest to northeast, along which storms follow a path which is more often than purely accidental. There is evidently something about the contours or the "lay of the land' which encouraged the winds to flow on these paths across the countryside. Sometimes, individual farms, located in the area of a tornado alley, will be hit more than once by storms following the path, in successive years.

Whether on the regular route of tornadoes or not, those families who get hit by a hard storm have the shock and wonder of going out around the farmyard to assess the damages. These may include one or more – or all – the buildings wrecked or completely gone, a windmill which is now a twisted tangle of steel struts, stacks of hay or straw scattered out across the landscape in a large streak, following the path of the winds. What may have been a tranquil grove of trees and "windbreak" for the farmstead, may itself be broken into a tangle of jagged sharp fingers of bright wood, with branches awry everywhere. And so, grateful for having come through with their skins, the farm family begins the task of building it all back again.

THE BLIZZARDS OF WINTER

There are few encounters with nature which are more forceful or direct than going through a blizzard on the plains of Dakota. It is important to understand the difference between a blizzard and simple snowstorm, however heavy a snow. A snowstorm is simply that – a storm in which a snowfall is thick and heavy – or thin and prolonged. It may have some wind with it or not. The snow may be light and fluffy as a feather or thick, heavy and wet, so the flakes are like tiny chunks rather than flakes. The temperature can even be warm – just below or above the freezing mark. But when all is said and done, it is still just a snowstorm.

A blizzard is a different animal. These earmarks that define a blizzard are my own creation but I think many people would agree with them in principle. First of all, temperature: the thermometer should be down around -20 or below, on to -40 F. There should be a gray, sullen overcast sky. There must be a high wind – the kind that shrieks and howls as it whirls around the corners of buildings – the kind of wind that would qualify as a windstorm, even if everything else was near normal. Finally, the snow. There must be a very heavy snow, driven by the high wind and broken by the cold into fine crystals – as fine as coarse flour – so that the snow can sift into cracks in a building wall or around a window or door and make tiny snow banks on the window sill. As a matter of principle, a proper blizzard should last for a day, overnight and into a second or even a third day before its towering anger has blown out and gone by. The snow should be so fine, like a white dust, that it shuts out visibility of objects even close by and can be so thick, it causes trouble in breathing.

There is no comfort like the assurances one can have in a snug, low house, with plenty of fuel for the stove, plenty of food in storage and plenty of blankets and quilts to make up a warm bed. Then, one can listen to the wind as it howls against the night – and crouch down in his safe retreat and let it blow. Pity the poor wretch who has to go out in it or <u>is</u> out in it, for we may not see him again in this life. <u>That</u> is a blizzard. So when a wimpy TV announcer excites over a "blizzard" that is slowing down traffic on I-?? somewhere, understand: he doesn't know what a blizzard is.

There were such storms, back in 1930 and 1920 – and on back into the 1880's. Almost every account of early life on the Dakota prairies mentions the classic Blizzard of 1888, which hit without warning on the mild morning of January 12. It set the standard by which later storms have been judged in this area, even to the present day. More than 500 people were frozen to death. Many pioneer family histories relate the loss of a relative or friends who did not make it through the Blizzard of '88. There were many people stranded in Vilas who had come in on the trains and were prisoners of the high winds, and temperatures at -40F.

There have been many blizzards since '88 – many which were very nearly as bad. There are accounts of pioneers who had to contend with snow drifts 10 and 20 feet deep. It was common for the early trains in this region to be stalled or stranded in heavy snow storms. There was another huge blizzard on June 12, 1910.

Large snow plows were attached to the front of the train engines. There is an account of a barrage of heavy chunks of frozen snow breaking out the windows of the Milwaukee depot in Vilas as a plow came roaring by, in a storm in the spring of 1916. In the early founding of Miner County, in the winter of 1880-81, no train was able to go from Madison to Howard in the entire time from February until June!

Livestock losses were enormous during some heavy storms and farmers were obliged to start over in the spring to re-build their herds. One can only try to imagine what life must have been like for the early homesteaders whose only shelter from the storm would have been a board claim shack or (better) a sod house, either with a dirt floor, no insulation, very little fuel and a "...board roof that let the howlin' blizzard in" as the folk song laments. At least, with that degree of shelter most survived but only barely.

They did what most of us would do: they did what they could to make it through. There were very cold winters in the 30's. January, 1936, was the fourth coldest month ever recorded in South Dakota. Ice on the Jim River was over two feet thick.

In the 20's and 30's, winters were not quite so grim. Most people had frame homes, however modest. Most people had horses in barns and sleds or cars, to get around once they dug themselves out. Digging out meant using a heavy scoop shovel to move the snow which would not be possible for most people today. Highway departments, both state and county, were primitive in their ability to clear roads and perform rescue missions as compared to today. A country road that was blocked by drifts often remained that way until the people who lived along the road went out with their shovels and dug themselves out. There were no skis, or snowshoes, or snowmobiles. One trudged on foot, from drift to drift.

For farmers, there was no electric heater to keep the ice off the water troughs for cattle and other animals. One had to go out and break through the ice with an ax to the still unfrozen water underneath.

In the face of such conditions, people of some decades back learned to prepare in advance for winter. The business of storing up food and fuel was real and much of it had to be done by the people themselves. Even if they had had the money, which most did not, they could not run to town and buy and bring home security. They had to provide it themselves.

In the years since, there have been many bad winter storms, with high winds, heavy drifting snow and temperatures down as low as -30 or more – so many such storms that no record remains in the public memory and they have been forgotten. But the word "blizzard" has a special meaning for people who lived in that era. The winters were more harsh and the present practice of calling every heavy snow storm a blizzard detracts from the definition of blizzards as being serious life-threatening storms. Nowdays, there are so many safety devices and systems in place that did not exist at all in the 20's and 30's.

The early winters were not all grief and hardship, of course. Most of the time, it was not blizzarding. People could go visit the neighbors. They could go to community dances and to church, albeit a struggle to get there by sleigh or early auto. But along with much else, most people today have no real understanding of what winter meant to the early citizens of the county. For the most part, they can be grateful that they have never had to learn.

A light buggy with springs and a padded seat.

Early touring cars carried luggage on the fenders.

PRAIRIE LIFE

STALKING THE STRIPED GOPHER

For boys growing up on the prairie in the 20's and 30's, hunting was a major diversion the year round. In spring and summer, it was gophers – 13 striped and flicker-tails. In fall and winter, it was jack and cottontail rabbits. Cottontails were by far the best if one intended to eat them. Fried cottontail, with mashed potatoes and gravy was hard to beat. Jackrabbits were hunted mainly because they were so plentiful. During a few years, the jack rabbits were so common they became a nuisance and hunting parties were organized of a dozen or more men who would conduct drives, herding the rabbits in the direction of the shooters, posted and waiting for them. Dozens and scores could be shot in a single day.

Small boys learned to hunt gophers at an early age, trying to snare them with a noose and a long string. With the noose fitted around the gopher's hole in the ground, one waited until he would stick his head up. Then, a quick pull would usually catch him and he could be pulled out of his hole and dispatched. Gophers were very common in the 30's – so much so that bounties were offered to boys who brought the tails to the Miner County Courthouse. Tails were worth five cents each, which was a small fortune in those austere times. A kid might collect .50¢ or even a dollar for a handful of gopher tails.

On one occasion, it was discovered that behind the courthouse, on an old ash heap, someone was dumping the gopher tails that had been brought in for bounty payments. This resulted in a brief bonanza for the kids who found them, for they simply took them back and collected a second reward! This went on briefly until the plot was discovered.

Gophers were caught in other ways. Some were "drowned out," when pails of water were poured down gopher holes. The residents below would appear quite promptly and they were set upon with clubs.

My world changed dramatically when I found a magazine ad offering a .22 rifle to boys who would pay $4.00 and sell 24 boxes of salve for chapped and cracked hands. My friend Bruce and I both answered the ad and received our boxes of salve to sell. We sold the salve mostly to our families and relatives at .50¢ a box. We sent the collected funds back to the salve company and within a couple of weeks, boxes arrived, containing – wonder of all wonders – a real, genuine Hamilton single shot bolt action rifle! They were kid-size rifles – perhaps 8 or 10 inches shorter than a normal .22. They were just right for us. We immediately made slings for them so we could carry them over our shoulders on our backs. We made leather pouches to carry our shells. One could buy .22 rifle shells for .20¢ a box (four gopher tails!). We were ready to face the wilds against all comers and for the next half dozen years, we did that: we roamed the fields and pastures – hill and dale – often from breakfast and until sunset. This all began when we were about 9 years old.

The idea of kids of that age armed with real rifles ranging the countryside would cause panic in many circles today. The kids would be captured and hauled before the authorities, along with their parents. In those days, it was the most ordinary thing in the world. No one gave it a second thought.

The ownership of that little rifle led to events that followed that had a profound effect in shaping my life. Going out to hunt crows or gophers or rabbits with my friend put me in the middle of the natural world almost daily. We became acquainted with the plants, grasses and weeds that covered the prairie. We learned their qualities – how they smelled and how they would taste if one chewed them, whether or not they were edible. We learned the trees, how they differed in appearance by bark, shape of leaves, characteristic form. We recognized the shrubs and bushes and the wild flowers. We learned the grasses and weeds and everything that grew. We roasted ears of corn over fires of willow sticks and chewed handfuls of ripe wheat, oats and barley. We drank water from the old iron pumps and windmills that were here and there on the cattle pastures. We saw the fox and coyotes, the badgers and skunks and weasels – and the snakes and lizards and toads and frogs – all the wild animals. We became wild creatures ourselves, in that we knew and felt at home with and understood the natural world around us. We came to know the coming changes in weather by looking at the sky. We watched the whirlwinds and the tornadoes blow by in the spring and summer. We felt the daily hot winds of the drought-ridden 30's.

We walked into the savage winds of winter – plodded through the drifts. We became reliant on our ability to find shelter in winter, shade in summer, where to look for food and water in the wild. All because of the little Hamilton rifle!

We were not hunters so much as residents of the countryside – we did not go out in the morning seeking to kill something – we went out to be in our true home. For me, the prairie was home. That was where I felt at home. What was emptiness and desolation to many was to me a place of feeling right about where one is – about being content and at peace with the surroundings.

So, I have a special affection for the hawks and owls that soar over the prairie, riding on the wind. I liked the crows – they are wiser than many humans and are resourceful beyond belief. I like the songbirds of the prairie – the Meadowlarks, above all, and the Bobolinks, the Redwings and the

Burrowing owls live in abandoned animal holes.

There are millions of striped gophers in South Dakota.

Meadowlarks are widely loved and are the de facto State Bird.

Photos by South Dakota Tourism

Yellowheads, the many sparrow-like little brownish–gray birds who flit about in the tall growth.

I liked to watch the swallows soar and sail around old railroad bridges and barns. If one came upon a grove of trees of any size, he would find woodpeckers, kingbirds, orioles, maybe tanagers and endless grackles. In a large grove and nearby grasslands, there would be from 25 to 40 species of birds in a season, if one kept a list of them.

There is much to be learned from paying attention to the bugs that crawl around in the grasses. Lying in a buffalo wallow, one may see in the grass a whole world of activity. There are ants of different sizes, beetles, grasshoppers and crickets, flies, gnats, bees and wasps – all going about their different kinds of business. And, one can stretch out and watch the clouds. There is much cause to wonder and stir the imagination. It is hard to imagine becoming bored on the prairie.

We spent a lot of time in native grasslands that had never been plowed. In the grass, there were scattered old white bones of buffalo and cattle bleached by many suns. There were patches of white sage that the Indians prized. There were large holes dug by badgers, coyotes and skunks. The large grey wolves were gone from the area but some were seen north of Howard in 1938.

There is nothing quite like a long drink of cool water from a pasture windmill when you are parched and dry from hours on the prairie. You drink a lot and you pour it over your face and arms and feet. Your body seems to soak it up, through the skin.

There were herds of cattle and we learned to size them up for we had real respect for the huge old herd bulls who might not like to have us around. We were chased by bulls more than once. One time, we ran into an especially grouchy big Hereford bull, who immediately started for us on a trot. We went on the dead run toward a nearby fence with him gaining ground behind us. Just as we got to the fence, we hit

The Coyote, Fox and Raccoon are about the prairie's most resourceful and enduring citizens.

Photos by South Dakota Tourism

the ground and rolled under the bottom barbed wire to safety. Happily, the bull stopped at the fence. Respect is learned from such experiences.

In the unplowed grasslands, there were many buffalo wallows, depressions about a foot or 18 inches deep, long grown over with short grasses. They were places where the buffalo rolled in the dust in summer, to rid themselves of pesky insects. Many of the bones bleaching in the sun were well preserved, along with buffalo horns. There were bones and horns scattered all across western Miner County, so it must have been a pasture regularly used.

At the end of the era of the buffalo slaughter, the prairie was littered with white bleaching bones. There were so many that they were gathered up by the settlers and piled in large "bone yards" and the large piles were loaded onto railroad cars and shipped to the eastern markets for use in factories. Cash-hungry settlers could make a few dollars selling the last remnants of the Old Frontier.

Small kids in the 20's and 30's sometimes played a game called "bone-yard" which had its origins in the era of bone collection. It was a game somewhat similar to the game of "Fox and Goose" which kids played in the snow in winter.

In the 20's and 30's, there were no large wild animals to be found in our area. I cannot remember ever having seen a single white-tailed deer, while today, they are common. There were no antelope – no cougars; bears and antelope had been gone for several generations.

ROCK CREEK BULLHEADS

Fishing in Miner County around Vilas was pretty sparse in the 1920's and 30's. The only place there were any fish in those years was in Rock Creek. Rock Creek was confined to fishing for bullheads and crayfish by kids. Adults wouldn't bother – they would go out to the Twin Lakes, southwest of Roswell or to Carthage or to Lakes Madison and Herman to the east. The catch was still confined to bullheads, perch and a few crappies – maybe a bass.

Fishing was one of the few recreational sports available to the farm people who made up most of the population. A family fishing expedition was an all-day affair. Mother would make up a lunch basket for a picnic along the shore, hopefully under a cottonwood tree on the grass. Fishing equipment was primitive beyond present-day imagination: fish poles were of bamboo, as long as 10 or 12 feet or more. Most fishing was done from shore and hence the long poles. In the busier locations, bait shacks sold minnows or worms and rented row boats (motors were generally unavailable). Fish line was made of tough cotton (nylon and other exotic plastics had yet to be invented). It was dark – usually black and heavy, which didn't seem to deter the fish at all. Fish hooks were plain and heavy. Lures were available for sale but few people used them since they were not after game fish; bullheads and perch were far more interested in edible bait anyway.

So, to fish, a hook was baited with a fresh live minnow or a fat, heavy earthworm or grub worm. A cork bobber was tied to the line at a distance above the hook so that the bait hung just above the bottom of the water.

Some days, one could fish – or sit – for hours without a nibble. Another day, the fish were hungry and could be hauled in about as fast as the hook could be re-baited and cast out with a swing of the long bamboo pole. Fish that were caught were often put into a gunny sack (made of hemp) and the sack laid in shallow water or hung over the edge of the row boat, to keep the fish alive until quitting time.

For my friends and me, fishing was a far less complicated business. It would always be in Rock Creek, for that was the only place close enough for us to go on foot. Why

Rock Creek was so named is not clear, for there really is no unusual number of rocks in or around the creek bed. Any other name would have served as well or better.

Rock Creek has its origin to the north, in Kingsbury County and flows southwest into the James River. A peculiar feature of the creek is that all of the small tributary creeks flow into it from the east and none from the west over its entire length. In the years of normal rain and snowfall, Rock Creek usually flowed until about midsummer when it would dry up into a series of separated pools.

The fish who lived in Rock Creek were fish that had swum upstream from the Jim and that had become trapped there when the summer flow dried up. These fish were mainly bullheads, carp, suckers and sunfish. Fishing usually took place during a day-long hunting trip which might include, gophers, mainly, but also jackrabbits and crows.

We always carried a small pouch on our belt or on a strap around our neck, which contained rifle shells and a sun glass (magnifier) with which to start fires by concentrating the sun's rays. And, there would be other items of utility for us, like leather strings or cords. For fishing we carried a length of black cotton fish line and a few hooks in a small package. To fish in the creek, we could cut a willow sapling for a pole, and use a piece of dry wood for a bobber and a piece of stone for a sinker. The water was never very deep – we would rarely find water holes in the creek where the water would be over our heads. More likely, it would be two or three feet or so. In times of real drought and no rain, sometimes the water would get down to a foot or less.

There were times when the creek was too shallow to fish with a pole. We would take off our shoes and wade into the water and catch some large bullheads with our bare hands! This was tricky and sometimes painful if one grabbed a bullhead in the wrong way and happened to grab him by the sharp, pointed "horns" on its head.

The fish were cleaned and cooked on the spot, on a spit over a small bonfire of willow or cottonwood. We sometimes roasted a pheasant that way too. On one occasion we even cooked a couple of crows, out of curiosity to see how they would taste. The meat was very strong and rank and disagreeable and we didn't need to eat much to learn that we didn't want to do that again!

A part of the charm for us to be along the creek was to see and become familiar with a variety of wild life – birds and animals that lived nearby and came to drink or feed in the water. In wide shallow wetlands along or near the creek, we saw many different small birds that probably most folks never saw.

One of the remarkable memories for me was a colony of Loggerhead Shrikes who lived in some locust trees and who would stick small animals – tiny mice and large grasshoppers – on the huge thorns that grew from the trunks and branches of these trees. We never saw the birds eat any of their victims – they seemed to have done it simply out of a perverse compulsion to kill and impale.

The most common big birds were the great blue herons, white egrets and rarely, night herons. Rarely seen but always heard in the dusk of evening was the mournful croaking cry of the American Bittern, a big brown, mottled bird with a long sharp bill, like a heron. In those days the only geese we saw were those coming and going in the spring and fall for they did not hang around the area all summer as some do now. There were ducks, of course, perhaps a dozen varieties.

There were lots of shore birds, like killdeers, cormorants, sandpipers and terns. The most exotic were the long-billed curlews, with their curved, five inch bills. They would fly so high in the sky they were like tiny specks against the blue and they had an eerie and peculiar cry.

We saw a lot of pied-billed grebes, locally called "mud-hens," that swam with a peculiar bobbing motion. About the size of a small duck, they were scorned by adult hunters as being unfit to eat. They may have been; we never tried them.

Bullheads were disdained by persons who regarded themselves as knowledgeable or skilled fishermen – they were the lowest on the totem pole of preference. It was said they had a strong or "muddy" taste. In fact, I have always felt that much of this disdain was a result of the feeding habits of bullheads who sought food along the bottom as do all the catfish family – and, because of their dark greenish-grayish, bluish color and general ugly appearance. They <u>looked</u> like a fish that would have an unpleasant taste!

Some farm families who had a successful fishing trip at one of the lakes might bring home a gunny sack full of fish and dump them in their stock tank near their windmill so they could be re-caught and prepared for the frying pan later on demand.

Another common resident of the area creeks was the crayfish or "crab." They were easily caught by tying bits of cut-up fish or other bait on a length of string and tossing it in along the creek bank. The crayfish would clamp onto the bait with his claws and then was hauled out and dumped in a bucket.

Crayfish were a sort of fresh-water shrimp and they were cooked in the same way: bring a kettle of water to boil, drop them in and when they turned red they were ready to pull out. Then, one broke off the tail (the only edible part) stripped off the shell and took out the dark vein. They looked like shrimp, tasted like shrimp and were every bit the equal of their salt-water cousins. They were a treat that was missed entirely by most local residents of that time, which is a great pity for they were a real delight.

Turtles were also common and one would see them floating on the surface with only their heads sticking out of the water, like little black plugs. Turtles were edible, too, but preparing them was quite a job. One had to take a chisel and cut off the bottom of the shell in order to get at the meat, which tasted something like chicken.

A plan was developed under the Works Progress Administration in 1934 to build two dams along Rock Creek. It was hoped that they could trap a permanent body of water to improve fishing and to develop recreational and picnic areas along the banks. Unfortunately, the 1934 dam washed out in the spring run-off. It was rebuilt, in a stronger version in 1935, but the dream of a recreational area never materialized for lack of rainfall and the dam gradually deteriorated.

CLOTHING

Among the things that have changed greatly since 1920 and '30 are the clothes people wore. There weren't many places where one could buy clothes then. One couldn't often jump in his Model T Ford and tear off to Mitchell or Madison or Sioux Falls to buy clothes – that was a major project. There were clothes to be bought in a couple of stores in Howard and one could even buy denim overalls and blue shirts in the Hepner Store in Vilas. But a great deal of clothing was bought from mail order houses like Montgomery Ward and Sears, Roebuck and Company. Nearly every family received these catalogs in the mail and they were pored over and pondered upon at great length. They had the advantage of allowing one to buy without being rushed into a decision, such as might be the case in a "live" store. Mail orders could be sent off with a money order purchased at the post office and the eagerly awaited package would arrive in a week or so.

The choices for clothing were much more simple then. There were no plastic artificial fabrics like nylon, orlon or any of the other "ons." There was only cotton, wool, linen and silk – all natural fibers. There were no zippers or Velcro-- only buttons and snaps. There were no light weight water and wind proof jackets and parkas; there were no parkas at all, for winter. The closest comparable winter coat would have been a sheepskin, with the leather turned out, and the wool on the inside. Caps were made of a heavy felt-like wool with "earflappers" that had strings on the ends to tie under one's chin. Thick woolen scarves were used to cover the throat and neck where the stiff, heavy coat couldn't reach.

Footwear was heavy and clunky. Heavy leather shoes and boots for winter and "tennis" shoes for summer – the forerunner of the infinite variety of sport, running, deck and lounging shoes now available. Waterproof overshoes and boots were made of pure rubber, with heavy metal buckles, or for dress, slip-ons. Open sandals and flip-flops were unknown for either men or women.

In general, women wore dresses – not pants. There were no jeans, as we know them now – only blue denim, bib overalls. Pants overalls could be found but they were not in general use, even by men. It would have been unseemly for a woman to wear pants on any regular basis. Stockings for both men and women were of cotton or wool, or silk for dress occasions.

A lot of clothing was home-made in those days. Women were much more likely to own and operate a sewing machine. Such machines were widely understood and good machines were passed down from mother to daughter, along with the knowledge of how to operate them. They were powered by foot pedals, although electric machines were beginning to appear. Electric ones were of little use anyway outside the towns for there was no electricity.

Women's and girls' dresses, skirts and blouses were cut from patterns sold in the general stores or from mail-order houses, out of cloth almost certainly bought in local "dry goods" stores. The stores stocked a great variety of threads and buttons and ribbons and other add-ons for the home seamstress.

Winter clothing in those days was far less suited to keep one warm. The overcoats were of heavy, felt-like material, hard to button and stiff and inflexible. They didn't really insulate so much as restrict motion. The soft, light-weight windproof parkas and coverall suits of today would have been only a dream then.

Similarly, the summer styles of today are much more relaxed. Shorts were not worn by men or women in Miner County. The summer dress of women today would have seemed daring and much too revealing. Nationally, change was afoot but it had not yet reached Vilas as yet.

One has to remember that these were days when money was scarce. Clothes were worn until they were worn out – in a large family, hand-me-downs were an absolute rule; - the little kids inherited items that were already well-worn by older siblings. It was harder to care for clothes, too. There were no dry-cleaning stores as are common now. If there were spots on one's vest, they would have to be rubbed out with cleaning fluids which one could buy or with soap and water.

The whole notion of "designer" clothing and attaching any importance to brand names would have been seen as absurd – these concepts had yet to be invented and sold to the public and they were of no influence then.

Clothes washing was as in another world. There were no automatic washers or dryers. There were no automats. Motors attached to washing machines were just beginning to be sold.

Washing machines were preceded by heating water in a large tub or kettle, clothes dumped in and stirred with a long wooden dowel and then lifted out and rinsed in tubs of cool water. Before hand-turned wringers, laundry was wrung out by hand.

The first washing machines were large wooden tubs, with an agitator powered by hand. The dryer was the outdoor clothes line in the backyard. Clothes were hung on clothes lines with wooden pins and carried back and forth in large wicker baskets. The washboard for scrubbing by hand and the wash tub and hand-wringer were still very well known.

Washing soaps tended to be harsh and powerful. Detergents were unknown. Soap meant bar soaps – even handmade, cooking animal fats and lye! Store-bought soaps were bar soaps or powders.

Scarcity and frugality meant one did not throw out worn or old clothing, too badly worn to be used any longer. Old cloth was converted to other purposes – recycled. One use for them was to make them into wash cloths and wash rags for all purposes. Both cotton and woolen goods were cut or torn into strips and made into braided rugs for the floor. Or, they were made into hot pads for the kitchen – or into something useful. And, there were no Salvation Army or Good Will collection spots to receive gifts for charity. Then, if you threw something out, it literally went to the dump.

There were virtually no knit clothes, such as tee-shirts and sweats; there were only sweaters and underwear. The only knit shirts for men were the white undershirts which gradually morphed into tee-shirts.

Public media had much less of an effect on people's clothing wants or choices. There was no TV, and far fewer movies, Sunday papers and magazines to fire the imagination. As there were fewer choices, so were there fewer devices to market clothes and build our want-lists. Faster and easier travel, communication and work saving machines have done much to speed change in what we wear.

WATER

In early prairie settlement days, getting water for drinking, cooking and for livestock was a difficult job. Outside of the large towns, there was no source except groundwater: a well. One had to dig, bore, drill or somehow get down into the ground to find water. The pioneer era was a time of opportunity for the well drillers. In still earlier times, wells had to be dug by hand, with spades and spuds and other such tools. The walls of a dug well shaft were sometimes lined with a masonry of broken field stone to prevent cave-ins. The arrival of the well drillers brought in a new era.

In Vilas there were very few wells. Most of the householders in the central part of the town relied on the "Town Pump." It was located about a block north of Main Street in the center of town. It had a windmill which pumped water most of the time; during times of calm and no wind, there was a long handle on the cast iron pump. One could unhook the long rod that ran down from the windmill gear box behind the fans up on the tower and pump his own water by hand.

Many families came to the well every day, with pails and jugs to fill them for use at home. It was a kind of gathering place for visits with the neighbors and to catch up on the local news.

There was an old man who brought a touch of Europe on his trips to the well. He came with two large pails suspended from a carved wooden neck yoke, which fitted over his shoulders and around his neck. One pail hung down on either side at arms length and he could hold the pail handles steady them and partly carry them with his hands as well as with the neck yoke. Two large pails of water were heavy and the yoke was important to help lift. It was supposed that he brought the yoke from Scandinavia, where he grew up. Oddly, no one else took up this good idea and made a yoke for himself, though he was a common sight, trudging up the street with his two pails of water. Change comes slowly, everywhere.

The Town Pump was a great place to gather for a drink of cold water fresh out of the ground. There was a large wooden water tank for horses, filled by a pipe from the pump. When the tank overflowed, the water drained away on a slope. Water ran through the pipe to the tank much of the time and one could cup a hand over the end of the pipe to catch a drink.

Every farm had a windmill and water tank for livestock. The stock tank served as a reservoir for water use all around the barn yard. Buckets were carried to fill troughs for drinking water for chickens, pigs and other animals and for whatever purpose water was needed.

In schools or public buildings, there were usually large covered stoneware jars for drinking water. It was common to find a long-handled dipper with which everyone could dip into the jar to get a drink! There was little or no concern about passing germs around through this common-cup process. The stone jars were filled by carrying pails from the nearest well.

There were no coin-fed machines dispensing drinks in the schools or public buildings. It was not possible to buy a bottle of water. There was no such thing. Everyone would have been scandalized at the idea of paying for a drink of water!

Today, all over Miner County, there are old steel windmill towers standing in the countryside, which mark the location of water wells. Sometimes, they are the only remaining vestige of what had been a farmstead, with house, barn and buildings. In the 1920's and 30's, these towers with a large circular array of fans at the top were everywhere whirling in the wind. The windmill was in universal use and made farming possible in the form that it was in those days. It was the only way available to get water for the household, the cows and other livestock and all other needs, unless it was all pumped by hand.

Wells drilled by the well drillers went deep into the ground and the hole was lined with pipe, called a well casing. Wells were drilled to varied depths, depending on the location of the underground water table. Most wells were about 100 or 200 feet.

The windmills themselves were of varied design. Very early ones had a wooden tower and fans and were short and stocky in appearance. More modern steel ones were much taller, to catch the winds that were stronger than those close to the ground.

Water from drilled wells was uniformly cold, coming out of the ground at around 54 degrees. Cool water was a welcome respite from the heat of the terrible, dry 30's with endless hot, southwest winds that blew from shortly after sunrise until sunset every day. Many windmills had a tin or granite-ware cup on a hook near the pump, to offer a cool drink for a passerby.

In the 1930's, when there was virtually no rain, some farmers ran pipes from the windmill pump to a nearby garden plot of fresh vegetables – tiny patches of green in a vast brown desert. Gardens distant from the house were watered from barrels hauled from the windmill on a wagon or stoneboat. Water was dipped with a small bucket to water the plants.

Before the days of indoor plumbing, all the water used in the home had to be hauled or carried by hand in pails and buckets from the windmill, in order to wash dishes, to fill the laundry tubs, to wash floors and everything, including the cream separator – the machine used to separate the cream from the whole milk. Finally, there was the water needed to wash hands and people, for baths on Saturday night (or however often they occurred). One could not turn a faucet to get water, not to say hot water. There were no faucets. Hot water was heated on a cook stove. Indoor plumbing and "running water" in the house were generally unknown.

Some families in both town and farm had another resource: rainwater. Some houses had large cisterns in the ground and lined with plastered concrete walls. Cisterns had concrete platforms on top with a large, cast iron manhole cover, large enough for a man to go down into it with a ladder. There was usually a cistern pump – a small iron hand pump to bring up the cistern water. Cistern water was soft rain water, free of the minerals often present in well water. Women prized it for washing hair, clothing finery and for watering house plants. It was not used for drinking since it often sat for months in the cistern, where insects and even an occasional mouse might have drowned.

Another option was the rain barrel. Both rain barrel and cistern depended on rainfall from the roof of the house, caught in eave troughs and drain pipes. Where there was little rain, water was the more prized and carefully rationed for only the most important purposes.

For farmers working in the fields, drinking water was carried in glass or stoneware jugs, wrapped in burlap, bound with binder twine. The jugs were filled with cold water at the windmill and then soaked in the stock tank to wet the burlap. Evaporation kept the drinking water cool. When the farmer reached the field, the water was placed in the shade of a tree or a wagon or inside a grain shock – anywhere to avoid the blazing sun.

Water was heated for bathing and for laundry in large tubs sometimes made of copper, on top of iron cook stoves or small laundry stoves. The stoves were fired with a variety of fuels: sticks of wood chopped from dead trees in a windbreak, or by corncobs saved from corn shelling, or coal if available from town. There were a few exceptions.

We lived in a house that did have running water, after a fashion. A pipe brought water from the well into a large metal cylindrical tank in the basement. A pump was attached to the tank with a long metal handle which was used to pump air into the tank. This created pressure which would force the water upstairs and to a large white enameled bath tub. It was the job of my brother and me, every day and sometimes several times a day, to go down and pump up the water tank, when the pressure was low. It was an onerous job but it was better than having to haul water in pails from the well.

Ice in early times came from blocks cut in nearby ponds or creeks with large metal saws like wood saws, but with much larger teeth – an inch or more long. Ice was hauled on sleds or wagons to the farm and buried in an oats bin in the granary or in a little shed filled with sawdust that served as an ice house. It remained buried in its insulated bed until summer when the blocks were hauled out to crack up and use in a hand-turned ice cream freezer or to cool pop or beer or other drinks. Ice handled in such a way would last through much of the summer. In later years, ice houses were maintained by the village general stores. Hepner's in Vilas sold blocks of ice.

Refrigerators with ice trays did not exist except in the towns where there was electricity, so for most people they were not available. An ancestor of the electric refrigerator was a heavy wooden cabinet called an "ice box" in which blocks of ice were placed to keep cool. A tray at the bottom caught water from the melting ice.

WHAT'S FOR DINNER?

Among the remarkable changes in prairie life brought about through science and technology has been in the foods people ate, where they got them and how they were prepared and preserved. Plastics were not yet in use and freezing was unknown. In America today, it is said that over half of all meals are eaten away from the home. That seems true for many people of Miner County – and most of the Northern Plains. In the 20's and 30's, there were fewer places to go to eat, away from the home. Then, far fewer women worked outside the home and most men were engaged in farm work. So in general, people ate their meals at home and the food they ate was prepared by themselves, from products they raised on their farms and in large home gardens.

Gardens were large and included sizable potato patches. Potatoes were planted in rows from seed potatoes prepared by cutting up selected potatoes in such a way that there would be one or more "eyes" on each piece. It was from the eye that sprouts grew to form the vines. The soil of the patch was prepared by plowing it up, with a horse-drawn walking plow, followed by a disc or drag to break up the large clods of dirt and smooth the surface. Most people then planted by digging a hole every two or three feet and dropping in two or three pieces of potato eyes. This would become what was called a "hill" of potatoes.

Once the potato plants had grown to a height of a foot or so, they would be assailed by potato "bugs" – small, hard-shelled striped beetles about the size of a large bean. Invariably, it became the job of the family kids to "pick potato bugs," by going along on hands and knees down the rows and picking off the bugs and dropping them into a large tin can about half full of kerosene. There was sometimes a pay scale of five or ten cents per each can of bugs.

Potatoes were dug with a garden fork to get a sampling of the first young tender ones. They were served in a white creamy sauce and – fresh from the ground – had a flavor that was distinctive and highly attractive. They were wonderful!

When the potatoes were fully grown, they were turned up with a plow, if in a large patch, and potato pickers followed behind on foot filling large baskets or containers.

The potatoes were stored in a potato cave or cyclone cellar, dug into the ground six or eight feet and covered over with timbers and dirt. These cellars often did double duty as a storehouse for root crops such as carrots, turnips, beets, parsnips and well as potatoes and as a refuge for the family when summer cyclones threatened.

Potatoes were a major staple food and were served boiled, mashed, baked, fried, and as the main ingredient in potato soups and salads.

Gardens contained other vegetables that were eaten fresh through the growing season. These would include peas and a variety of beans, and cucumbers for pickles, rhubarb, cabbages, kohlrabi, sweet corn and other edibles. There were herbs for seasoning, like dill for pickles and sage for stuffing holiday turkeys or pork roasts.

All of these varied plants seemed to have special bugs and insects that appeared when they did – heaven knows how the bugs knew. Some of the larger ones – beetles – that attacked the beans could be dealt with like the potato bugs: pick them off each plant by hand and drown them in kerosene. For the other bugs, there were no invented chemical poisons as are now common and the plants had to be sprayed with what are now considered to be organic bug poisons – there were often home-made mixtures as well.

Tomatoes were a major garden crop. Plants were started from seeds saved from the season before and planted in early spring in window boxes in enclosed porches and even inside the home. Large plates of fresh, red tomato slices were a part of everyday menus in the summer.

During the great drought of the 1930's, some family gardens were saved by irrigation from the windmill or the pump driven by small stationary engines, hooked up with a pump-jack which was a device to raise and lower the pump's piston to raise up water, in the same way a windmill would. Because of the water in the tiny ditches, they attracted small song birds and animals including garter snakes who liked to lay in the cool damp spots under the plants.

A big garden helped provide a bountiful table during the growing season but its major purpose was to produce foods that could be preserved by canning and drying, to eat during the winter ahead.

Canning was women's work and was on-going through the seasons of the various crops as they would ripen on their schedule. Canning required the knowledge of the qualities of each different product, as to how to prepare it. Sometimes, neighbor women would band together to help each other and to enjoy each other's company.

Canning meant picking and washing the vegetables, and cutting them up with kitchen knives into appropriate sizes, then cooking them in kettles on top of the large iron cook stoves. When ready, the cooked items were filled into an array of sparkling, clean glass jars, sterilized by boiling. Rubber rings, gaskets and tops were set on tightly and the jars put away in pantries or basement shelves. Some crops like peas and beans were canned green and dried, by picking the pods from the dried vines in the fall, shucking the beans into containers to store for winter when they would be converted into kettles of soups or other dishes.

There were other delights coming from the garden, which included strawberries, raspberries, currants, gooseberries and ground cherries. From bushes and small trees came sand cherries, choke cherries, plums, apples, pie cherries, and rarely peaches and pears. All of these could be canned as whole fruits or converted into a great variety of jellies, jams and syrups. Everyone had a rhubarb patch, to make the world's most wonderful pies and crisps, toppings and sauces.

One of the benefits of being a harvester of fruits was that one could eat some of the best specimens as he went along: a large and lush berry might never make it to the kitchen to be canned.

Still other bounty from the gardens included sweet corn to be eaten boiled on the cobs, or to be canned and/or cut off the ears and dried. And, the melons – water, musk, cantaloupe – and the pumpkins for pies and Halloween and the gourds and sweet potatoes.

While it made wonderful eating, the raising, processing and preserving of all of these foods was a lot of work but it was taken for granted – that was how things were done and were really not an option, if one were to eat!

The foods available in the stores in those years were limited to canned goods or fresh foods. There were no frozen foods and packaged dry items such as cake mixes and supplements to meat dishes as now common. The canned foods were limited pretty much to pork and beans, a few soups, fruits, such as peaches or pears. Today's super food markets would have been inconceivable. Besides, it was considered wasteful to spend scarce cash money for foods that could be prepared at home – cash was hard to come by.

Bread is an example. Nearly all women baked breads, biscuits and rolls as often as weekly – even daily. It was wonderful bread, much more substantial than store-bought bread, which was available but was seen as so soft and light and effete one would only buy it for novelty's sake. Bread came to the grocery stores in big wooden boxes with many loaves in each and they were wrapped by the grocer for the customer.

Desserts were generally forms of cake and pies. Pie making is now largely a lost art, and good examples are found today mainly in the dinners sponsored by Ladies' Societies in the churches. It is really not possible to get a good piece of pie in a restaurant or in a super market; their crusts are especially bad in most cases. Pies were made of lots of things in the prairie kitchen. Unknown today are pies made of ground cherries and of "stubble berries" which was a local name for the small dark, blue-black berries that grew on low bushes in the fields of grain stubble and were ripe for picking after the harvest in the fall. They were wonderful for pies. Of all, rhubarb, fresh-cut and into the oven with a light flaky crust, has no peer in the world!

Fruit "sauces" were often served as a dessert. They were simply fresh or canned sliced fruits, often in their own sugary syrup. Doughnuts and cookies were common and nearly always homemade.

Virtually all butter was made at home from cream separated from milk and churned in a hand-cranked churn which held about a gallon. From this came wonderful butter and buttermilk as well. Butter was – with lard – the principal fat used in cooking, for the inventions and substitutes from the chemistry labs had not yet hit the market.

Meats were processed and prepared at home. People who lived in towns and had no livestock bought their supplies of meats from farm acquaintances or relatives. Groups of neighbors banded together to form "meat rings" for butchering beef, pork or other animals, with each family receiving a share of the meat produced.

Beef, pork and lamb all came from the annual process of butchering of animals chosen and specifically fed and cared for by the farmers. Roasts, chops, steaks, bacon, sausages, spare ribs – whatever – all came from the same processes.

Butchering hogs was the most complicated. The hog was slaughtered and the internal organs removed – though the heart, liver and possibly the kidneys were saved for special preparations, as was the tongue of beef cattle. With pigs, the hair had to be removed and so a huge iron kettle was set up and a tripod with a rope block and tackle attached. By this means, the pig was raised and lowered into the boiling water to loosen the hair. It was then placed on a wooden table or platform and the hair removed with large scrapers. Next the process began of cutting and slicing out the hams, roasts, chops, ribs, stew meat, steaks and other cuts.

Fresh meats were set aside for immediate use and the rest went for preservation. Hams and bacon were placed in large stoneware crocks in between layers of salt and salt water and they might be placed in a smoke house to be cured by smoking. The smoke house was a small wooden building with iron hooks around the walls and on rafters overhead on which slabs of bacon or hams could be hung. In the floor of the building was a wood fire of smoldering coals. Different woods gave off varied flavors; hickory, apple and other woods were used as available. Some households preserved pork chops in stone crocks filled and covered with lard; the meat was dug out of the lard as needed.

All meats could be canned and chunks of cooked beef or pork were sealed up in glass jars with tallow or fats and juices and later opened to provide a marvelous gravy for mashed potatoes.

Sausages of great variety – often of ethnic origins – were produced, using special grinders and casing stuffers to prepare them. They too, might be smoked. Heavily seasoned ground pork was made into breakfast sausages and preserved in lard crocks.

The fat trimmed from the pork butchering was itself cooked up in a large iron kettle outdoors, over a fire, to cook the fat out of the meat and produced lard, which was stored in stone crocks.

Ethnic recipes – handed down from ancestors who came from north Europe produced a great and novel variety of meat dishes, such as head cheese (from pig's head) and the pickled knuckles of pig's feet. Sliced beef tongue was considered a delicacy by many. Liver was fried with onions and liver, converted into a kind of wurst or sausage, was common.

Today, we need to consider and should marvel at all of the special knowledge and skills that were required to make all of these varied preparations of meat for the table. The how-to-do-it information was passed down through the family from the old to the young and represented accumulated learning of prior centuries. Today, we go to the market and buy all of these products with dozens of variations and take their availability for granted. The prairie people had to know how to do it themselves and spend many days every year in the process.

In general, the diet of the rural prairie people was one that would serve people who worked physically hard every day, from dawn to dusk. Everything they did was labor-intensive and required muscle. Many nutritionists today would be scandalized at the content and the portions of their meals. But it was a different society and a very different world in many ways, in the 1920's and 30's.

THE PARTY LINE

Telephones were in fairly general use on the farms and in the small towns but they were a far cry from the telephone magic of today. In the 20's and 30's, telephones were nearly all in the form of a large wooden box usually made of oak. It measured about ten inches wide and perhaps 18 inches high. It was mounted on the wall and one would stand in front of it to talk into a mouthpiece the size of a teacup which stuck out in front. There was a receiver on a wire, about the size of a one pound dumbbell, to hold against the ear.

A crank on the side of the box was used to "ring up" the live operator in a telephone office in a nearby town. The operator was told the number being called – or even the name of the person – and she would manually plug in the caller to a switchboard to connect to the person being called.

Left: At the center of early phone systems was the operator who plugged in connections by hand.

Below: Bananas hang in a general store in the 1920's.

The caller might well converse with the phone operator in passing, to learn some local news or give some, to pass along. Persons on the phone line would hear the rings on their phone and, out of curiosity take down the receiver to see what the call was about! This process of listening to a neighbor's phone calls was called "rubbering" and was a very common practice among the farm wives of the area. So much for current concerns about invasion of privacy! Sometimes, there were so many neighbors rubbering on the line, that the phone line was drained of electrical energy. The call would become so weak, those conversing could not hear each other! Then, the caller would make sharp requests for people to get off the line so the call could continue!

Phone lines were rather simple systems, with the wires strung on wooden posts and tied to green glass insulators with wire. These insulators have become an item of interest in antique markets in recent years.

GYPSY CARAVANS

A summertime happening in South Dakota communities in the old days that has since vanished entirely was the arrival of the Gypsy caravans. Few events provided more excitement or raised more curiosity or provided more uneasiness and wonder. Gypsies had been coming through the countryside ever since there were enough settlers there to provide a challenge for them. They were skillful beggars and fortune tellers and there were always local people who were captured in it all.

The Gypsies traveled in a column of wagons, accompanied by a drove of horses. These wagons were often elaborate, a sort of combination of a stage coach and a patent medicine seller's wagon. They were sometimes elaborately carved (the woodwork) and with painted decorations. For nearly everyone, they carried as cargo an aura of mystery.

The Gypsies traveled the back roads – the dirt section line roads – both to avoid traffic with their imposing array of wagons and horses and sometimes, riders and walkers and, to allow them access to the farmsteads located in almost every mile along the road. At the farms, they could stop and beg, buy or steal needed items: water, chickens, eggs, milk, butter, meats and vegetables in season. And, they could trade horses with the farmers who were willing. They knew horses and they were shrewd traders – it was a rare farmer who got the better of a horse trading deal. The back roads provided them places where they could pull over and set up camp for the night in a pasture or grove of trees where they could have a measure of privacy, away from the eyes of the curious.

The Gypsies themselves were a collection – one could call them a tribe or a band – of families and extended families – people of all ages – little kids – old people, and the main body of able-bodied adults. There seemed to be a large number of middle-aged women, large – heavy and buxom, who were dressed in a welter of layers of dresses, scarves, hoods and other mysterious coverings. One had the impression of a large bundle of varied clothes.

The Gypsies were dark-skinned – sort of an olive-tan – dark hair and eyes. Among themselves, they spoke a language foreign-sounding and strange, which added to the sense of mystery that surrounded them.

One could see a band of Gypsies coming for some distance away – their caravan moved slowly which allowed people who saw them coming to scurry around and secure their belongings, lest the Gypsies should stop in and pay them a visit, for they were notoriously light-fingered and almost anything of value could disappear as they swarmed over a country farmstead.

One drowsy, hot summer afternoon, a large band came into the town of Vilas – came down the main street and stopped in front of Hepner's General Store. A large number of women – they with the many cloaks and dresses – invaded the store. Another small boy and I were in the store. The only person minding the store was Mrs. Hepner, wife of the owner. The Gypsy women fanned out quickly going into every aisle and display area. They filled the many pockets in their many dresses with goods of every description – needles, thread, buttons, kitchen knives and house wares, small items of hardware, small packages of food, items of clothing – whatever was small enough to fit into or under the many layers of clothing they wore. Mrs. Hepner saw it all happening – she was frantic but unable to do anything to stop the thieves – there were too many and on all sides. Then, suddenly, like a swarm of predator bees, they all turned and left the store with their plunder, jumped into the wagons and the caravan pulled quickly away, leaving the stricken Mrs. Hepner and two wide-eyed little boys.

There was no way to stop the Gypsies. There was no constable or law officer in the town and one law man would have been helpless anyway. There was no group of men at hand who could have been formed into a posse to give pursuit. The Hepners were simply out of all the items taken from the store with no way to recover.

In those years, it was not unknown for older members of a family to threaten misbehaving kids, that "if they didn't behave, they would be given to the Gypsies!" Or, that if they did do thus or so, Gypsies would come and kidnap them and haul them away! It was a fairly effective deterrent to mischief among small kids.

The Gypsies kept to themselves. They wanted no part or association with the resident populations among whom they traveled. Their life and culture was too different and far removed. On a summer evening, their campfires, the smell of wood smoke, the buzz or talk and sometimes song, was not unlike the camp of any band of vagabonds, in any time or place.

Gypsies were quite common – every summer brought one or more visits. As time went on and horse travel gave way to motor cars, they gradually vanished from the scene.

ITINERANT PEDDLERS

There were others beside Gypsies who traveled through the farm communities, to bring goods for sale to the farm families. There were peddlers – salespeople – of varied description – selling a wide range of different things. In the horse and buggy days – generally earlier than the 1930's – peddlers came with goods for sale to the farm women - bolts of cloth, needles, thread, buttons, yarns and knitting needles, ribbon, all kinds of items useful for sewing clothing, window curtains, bed linens – all the many things that rural women made for the home and family.

There were other salesmen as well – some selling lightning rods to place on top of barns and farm buildings, which were supposed to attract lightning during thunderstorms and conduct it down to the ground and avoid burning the building. Some salesmen developed highly skilled and slick sales talks to hypnotize farmers into the purchase of kits of lightning rods and cables of doubtful quality and value. The description of a seller as being "slick as a lightning rod salesman" became a kind of by word in the region.

The summer always brought other salesmen – selling supplies for the rural kitchen: peppers, spices and herbs and extracts of vanilla and various flavors for cooking. There were lines of patent medicines, first aid items, salves, lotions and toilet waters.

The most notable and reputable of these salesmen were the representatives of the Rawleigh and Watkins companies, whose representatives sometimes followed routes of call over many years. Central Miner County was served by a Rawleigh products salesman named Fred Formanack of Roswell. There were many other salesmen of cookware, pots and pans and all sorts of kitchen hardware and knick-knacks. Others sold Bibles, books or correspondence courses for self-improvement in a wide range of fields, and these were often welcomed since education was not as readily available in those times.

In the middle to late summer, peddlers came with trucks loaded with the wonderful Forestburg melons – watermelons and muskmelons. Some, like Louis Schwemle of Forestburg, were widely known and trusted on the farms. Melon salesmen were always willing to cut out a "plug" – a triangular sample about an inch wide – or sometimes, to cut open an entire melon and pass around samples to the gathered to impress them with the flavor and quality.

Prior to World War II, and especially during the Depression of the 1930's when no one had any money, it was common for the salesmen to take chickens in exchange for their goods – a kind of barter system in which a given number of chickens would equal a given number of dollars. The salesmen would have several chicken crates tied on to the back bumper of his car and he and the farm wife and kids would run around the chicken yard catching chickens and putting them in a gunny sack for transfer to the crates on the car. When the crates were full, the salesman would then have to journey to the next nearest buyer of poultry to convert the chickens into cash.

Life moved at a much slower pace in those days. A visitor, even in the form of a salesman, was often welcome on the remote farm. He brought news, gossip of the neighborhood and the region around. He represented a touch with the outside world. He was a break in a routine that would have been more burdensome without him.

COMMUNITY DANCES

Public dances were major sources of entertainment and served as a social commons during the 1920's and 30's. Dancing had always been a means of getting acquainted and letting off steam since the earliest settlement days, when dances were held in homes, barns and public halls. Dances were regularly held in the warmer months – especially in summer – in the IOOF Hall in Vilas, the Legion Hall in Howard, in Winfred and in the Dane Hall about 3 1/2 miles south of Vilas. There were dances in Fedora, Argonne, Carthage, Artesian, and nearly every other community.

It was during the early 30's that the era of the Big Bands and Swing Music rose up in America. This lead to the forming of regional and local dance bands who played the new popular music in places like Lake Madison, Oldham and Ruskin Park, out on the Jim River.

Ruskin Park was probably the most notable of these dance halls for it attracted Lawrence Welk of WNAX in Yankton and some of the largest area bands such as Jimmy Barnett, whose reputation extended over the region from Omaha to Denver to Minneapolis. Ruskin Park was the name attached to the former McFarld Grove, a natural wooded park area along the James River southeast of the town of Forestburg. It was established in 1903 and provided space for picnicking, a tenting area and a group of summer cottages. There was a gasoline launch on the river to provide rides for visitors. There were feature baseball games, such as Sioux Falls vs. Platte and there were airplane rides, in barnstorming biplanes. It was a very popular resort for many years and provided a large dance hall which attracted young adults from fifty miles in every direction.

Groups made popular by radio shows from Sioux Falls, like Curly Boyd and the Dakota Cowboys and New Ulm's Six Fat Dutchmen, were well attended.

Some of the dances in country halls on Saturday nights became quite spirited, with bootleggers supplying moonshine out of auto trunks in the back of the hall. Emboldened and freed of convention, hot-headed swains engaged in fist fights, in contention for the favor of the more attractive young women. Such locations sometimes were visited unexpectedly by the county sheriff in search of bootleggers and to provide a semblance of order.

Music for barn dances and country dance halls was provided by local area musicians, composed usually of a piano, one or more fiddles and guitars, perhaps a drummer, trumpeter, saxophone or clarinet player.

The pattern of events for the evening followed a fairly regular pattern. Dancing began about 8:00 p.m. Bands would play a sequence of sets of three or four pieces, with brief intervals in between for dancers to change partners and briefly rest. This went on until sometime approaching midnight, when the band would announce an "intermission." Dancers would go to their autos to have a few shots to reinforce their happiness and/or to do some romancing. The music would begin again after a half-hour break and continue until about 1 a.m., after which some dancers would again resort to the cafes to roister and party until some time later in the night.

People attending the dances tried to appear in their best clothes and to be as clean and fashionable as possible, since many of the dancers were single and were there to attract the interest of potential partners.

As with everything else, the rise of better cars, roads, telephones and radios, the character of the music gradually changed and spread the patterns of behavior common in urban areas.

BOOTLEGGERS

An on-going thread in the area culture in the 1920's and early 30's was a sub-rosa activity generally called "bootlegging." Bootleggers were persons who sold home-made alcohol to party-goers and celebrants. They either made it themselves or bought from people who were operating a "still" for making booze. There were a number of bootleggers in Miner County in those years, located mainly on the western side of the county, around Carthage and Argonne. The wooded valleys along the Jim River to the west in Sanborn County was a notorious location for stills and lairs of rustlers and horse thieves.

My grandfather, G. F. "Gus" Kilian was sheriff of Miner County in 1925. One of his chief occupations was chasing bootleggers and raiding stills. He confiscated lots of "goods" from time to time, together with tubs and boilers and other gear used in cooking up moonshine. There is a round copper boiler about 18 inches high which was taken by him that came from a substantial still in northwest Miner County.

The bootleggers who were the most professional in their work bottled up the alcohol in small clear half-pint flask-shaped bottles and even packed them in cardboard boxes with little paper dividers.

Bootleggers found a lively market at the dance halls around the county. They would pull up behind or on the dark side of the building and sell bottles out of their car trunk. The appetite for booze was reliable and constant at those dances, and sometimes found extreme expression. The story was told of an event that happened at a country hall, where a thirsty swain, desperate for some stimulation, lay down under the radiator of an auto, turned the petcock to drain it and caught the alcohol in his mouth! We may assume he lived to tell the tale though alcohol as an antifreeze was not for human consumption.

Bootleggers were a product of the national laws on Prohibition. In the 18th Amendment to the federal constitution, sale of alcohol beverages was illegal. Prohibition came to an end during the presidency of Franklin D. Roosevelt with the repeal of the 18th Amendment.

Homemade alcoholic beverages were fairly common. Grandfather Kilian, of German descent, decided that he was going to make a batch of home-made beer. He set up his modest brewery in the basement and installed cases of new glass bottles, a machine to cap the bottles and various tub-like containers to brew the beer in. He went through all of the motions, brought the beer to the proper stage, put it into the bottles, and set them on the shelves. But something went wrong. One quiet Sunday afternoon, the bottles began to explode – to blow up. The caps could be heard hitting the ceiling with a snap. There was foam and froth and beer all over the floor, shelves and walls. Grandmother Kilian, who wasn't excited about the project to begin with, was not amused. She made Grandpa clean up his mess and he never tried it again.

TWIN LAKES

One of the projects of the Federal Works Progress Administration was the construction of a recreational area called the Twin Lakes, about half a mile west and a mile south of the town of Roswell. Twin Lakes was a natural area of two adjoining lake beds, left from the glacial periods that formed the plains in Miner County. The WPA built what may have been its most ambitious project in Miner County. Large artesian wells were drilled on the south end of the two lakes and water gushed in heavy streams to fill the lake beds with clear fresh water. In the hot, dry years of the 1930's, this was a powerful attraction.

The project included the building of an area for a public swimming beach with sand hauled in to make the beaches and a large tower with diving boards was installed. There was an island on the north side of the south lake and a causeway, built of field stones and heavy gravel, which allowed foot traffic to and from the island.

Some small private wooden buildings were put up to house hamburger stands and other vendors; a dance hall was built which was an immediate success. It was a low wooden frame building with windows at the sides. On at least one occasion, a surprise visit by the county sheriff in search of illegal alcohol resulted in some young dancers bailing out the side windows to escape arrest and hiding in the adjoining trees and fields until the coast was clear.

Fishing for bullheads and perch flourished at Twin Lakes, for the bullheads multiplied quickly with no larger predator fish to gobble up the young.

Sunday afternoons were especially popular at Twin Lakes, with whole families coming to picnic, fish, swim and generally hang out. It was a very attractive place for young people. Girls had a place to show off the most fashionable and daring new swim suits and the boys had a place to come and ogle. Old folks could sit in the shade and visit or tend bamboo fishing poles set up for bullheads. Young kids could jump off the lower diving boards and make a great splash.

Time causes everything to modify and change. The coming of the Second World War spelled the end for Twin Lakes. The flow from the artesian well slowed down and the wells were eventually capped. The buildings were torn down and hauled away to be recycled. Today, one can drive by on the curvy road of the east side of the lakes and find only an un-

Twin Lakes swimming beach, dance hall and varied concessions attracted hundreds during summer weekends.

Large pipes from flowing artesian wells filled the lakes and made it all possible.

tended grove of shade trees. There is nothing left of the old summer resort on the ground to show that it ever existed. The peals of youthful laughter and the splashing of the swimming pool have all drifted off into space, to wherever sounds of the past go.

Twin Lakes became a game production area under the guidance of the State Department of Game Fish and Parks, in 1948. It is a good place to watch for birds – especially water and shore birds. Ducks, coots and herons are common. Pelicans often pull in for a visit. Owls and hawks hang out in the trees along with woodpeckers, kingbirds and all of the small birds of the prairie. So now, Twin Lakes is a place where one can find solitude and quiet nature, rather than seek company and noisy companionship. Then and now are very different times.

SATURDAY NIGHTS IN HOWARD

One of the most widespread customs of the prairie people in the 20's and 30's was their uniform behavior on Saturday night. Most farmers – especially the younger families with kids – went to a town that was the trade center of the area on Saturday night. This was an important ritual – they looked forward to it all week. It was a combined social and economic outing – the most important, unexciting thing was to shop at the grocery store and buy the things needed for the days ahead and, also to shop in the clothing and hardware stores.

For the people in central Miner County, the town was Howard. It was the place one HAD to be if he were a young person. People would drive their cars into town early to make sure they got a preferred parking spot in the central area of Main Street. Why? Because in the course of the evening, from late dusk until midnight or after, people walked up and down the sidewalk and one could sit in his car and watch this procession – one could see who was there and who wasn't. This was especially important for the high school girls, who dressed in their finest summer attire and in parties of two or three or four, walked up and down the sidewalks in front of the principal stores and shops, (and in front of all the people watching in the parked cars!). They would go around and around, up one side and down the other, feigning interest in the shop windows and stopping to talk, with great animation, with passing friends. The main point of all this was to make certain that the boys who they hoped to interest saw them!

There were other activities: a large old fashioned popcorn wagon on the southwest corner of Main Street and Farmer did a land-office business on Saturday nights, serving up fresh popped corn and big gobs of real butter. At several doors south on the west side of Main Street was the Grand Theatre, later called the Paradise, which ran movies for two shows. People could go to the "first" or "second" show and thus arrange the balance of their schedule for the night.

The elders, quiet subdued farmers in their freshly washed bib-overalls, stood in little knots along the curb, or sat on the fenders of their cars, talking shop and trading opinions about whatever was of current interest. Their wives were more likely to congregate in the aisles of the stores or even in the several small main street cafes, for coffee or a sundae.

The girls wore light summer dresses or blouses and skirts with white shoes. The boys who were watching them – and also hoping to get noticed – uniformly wore white shirts with the sleeves rolled up above the elbow, and light colored or white pants and, if they had them, white or highly polished shoes.

Farmers used the trip to town to dicker with machinery and auto dealers as well as to bring in the weeks production of eggs and cream, to trade for groceries.

The movies at the Paradise were generally shoot-'em-up Westerns, with stars like Hopalong Cassidy or Roy Rogers. There were always short subjects, little travelogues or reports of news around the world (there was almost always a news feature) and there were comedies. The first cartoons of Disney-like characters were just beginning to appear. Occasionally, there were current musicals with stars like Bing Crosby and Bob Hope and comedies with the Marx Brothers, Jimmy Durant and many others. Some really important films were shown – like Gone With the Wind, with Clark Gable. All of these could be seen for a ten cent ticket – a wonderful age!

All of this was reserved for the magic warm nights of summer. Wednesday nights were a much smaller version of Saturday night: the high school band often played a concert on a band stand on wheels that was rolled up onto the center of Main Street. These concerts went on into the very late summer, when the really bright northern lights of that era appeared overhead before the concert was over. There were ten cent movies on Wednesday nights, too.

One of the real attractions of those nights was the legendary food: hot crisp hamburgers, with catsup and pickles and chips, and the sensational chocolate malts at the drug store soda fountains. There were two drug stores directly across the street from each other: Rafferty's and Klein's – and each made wonderful malts. There were little ice cream parlor tables with marble tops and chairs with backs of metal hoops. It was authentic Americana in every way. It was a time for young swains who had cars to persuade the more daring girls to go for rides. And if one didn't have a car, to persuade them to go for walks on the darker streets, up to Nobles' Park and back.

Dances were a more important feature of the social life of those decades than now seems true. The kids of Howard's high schools – both the pubic school and the Catholic St. Ag-